Shenandoah
NATIONAL PARK
Official Handbook

Shenandoah

NATIONAL PARK

Official Handbook

By
Anne Mitchell Whisnant, Ph.D.
David E. Whisnant, Ph.D.
Tim Silver, Ph.D.

The Donning Company Publishers
184 Business Park Drive, Suite 206
Virginia Beach, VA 23462

Cataloging-in-Publication Data

Whisnant, Anne Mitchell.
  Shenandoah National Park official handbook / by Anne Mitchell
Whisnant, David E. Whisnant, Tim Silver.
      p. cm.
  Includes bibliographical references.
  ISBN 978-1-57864-670-8 (softcover : alk. paper)
  1. Shenandoah National Park (Va.)--Handbooks, manuals, etc.
2. Shenandoah National Park (Va.)--Description and travel. 3.
Shenandoah National Park (Va.)--History. I. Whisnant, David E.,
1938- II. Silver, Timothy, 1955- III. Title.
  F232.S48W44 2011
  975.5'9--dc22

                                    2011016160

Printed in the United States of America at
Walsworth Publishing Company

Credits:

Shenandoah National Park Staff:
Martha Bogle, Wendy Cass, Claire Comer, Jennifer Flynn, Dan
Hurlbert, Sally Hurlbert, Ann Kain, Neal Lewis, Karen Michaud,
and Gordon Olson

John Amberson, Shenandoah National Park Volunteer

Greta Miller, Shenandoah National Park Association

Photos on front cover and pages 65, 81, 82–83, 105, 119, 163,
169, 170–171, provided by Ann & Rob Simpson
Photo on 119 by Ed Knepley

TABLE OF CONTENTS

FOREWORD

PART I: NATURAL HISTORY
by Tim Silver, Ph.D.

PART II: CULTURAL HISTORY
by David and Anne Whisnant, Ph.D.

PART III: EXPERIENCE SHENANDOAH TODAY

Foreword

FROM YELLOWSTONE TO SHENANDOAH:
BRINGING NATIONAL PARKS TO THE EAST

Until 1919, nearly a half-century after the birth of our first national park (Yellowstone, 1872), "National Park" meant a large park located somewhere in the western states. Anyone from east of the Mississippi who wanted to visit a national park had to travel at least a thousand miles to do so.

To be sure, traveling such a long way rewarded visitors with vast arrays of spectacular scenery: canyons, geysers, waterfalls, glaciers, mountains, volcanic landscapes, and dramatic geological formations. But at length the problem came to be that nearly two-thirds of the U.S. population lived in the East, with the center of population lying forty miles southwest of Indianapolis.

Attention to the imbalance began soon after the birth of the National Park Service. Its first director Stephen Mather began to encourage the building of parks in the East, partly to shore up Congressional support for the still young federal agency. "I should like to see," Mather wrote in his 1923 annual report on the national parks, "additional national parks east of the Mississippi.... There should be a typical section of the Appalachian Range established as a national park...."

Mather's suggestion resonated within the southern Appalachian region. More than twenty years earlier, in 1899, leaders from southern, western, and New England states had organized the Appalachian National Park Association (ANPA) to push for a national park in the Blue Ridge or Great Smoky Mountains. A report from the secretary of agriculture in 1901 put the federal position clearly: EASTERN STATES ARE ENTITLED TO A NATIONAL PARK.

The ANPA's urgency was impelled partly by rapacious logging in the mountains. Western North Carolina, eastern Tennessee, Virginia, and West Virginia were being timbered relentlessly. The Hassinger Lumber Company opened huge operations on 30,000 acres in Virginia's Washington County in 1905, and by the 1920s, industrial loggers had clear-cut nearly 60 percent of the Great Smoky Mountains area. Much of what loggers left, fires and floods finished off.

ANPA's efforts were widely applauded, but they were also strongly resisted by lumber interests. The lumbermen, opposed to removing lands from logging, preferred national forests—where cutting was permitted—instead of parks. Confronted by this opposition, the southern Appalachian park movement took a new form as a movement for a southern Appalachian forest preserve. Public pressure continued, however, and eastern parks began to be authorized and developed.

Part I

NATURAL HISTORY

By Tim Silver, Ph.D.

Chapter I

LIVING LANDSCAPE

On a late May evening at Big Meadows, it is easy to forget that the rest of the world exists. Does accompanied by wobbly-legged fawns emerge from the forests to browse the wide expanse of grassland. Songs of cardinals and wood thrushes gradually give way to the plaintive warbles of screech owls. A thin white mist—the remnant of an earlier rain shower—rises slowly from the landscape as darkness envelops the gray ridges in the distance. When the evening chill sets in, visitors retire to the sitting room in Big Meadows Lodge and settle into rocking chairs, enjoying the fireplace and watching the moon rise through giant picture windows. It is a time to savor, to be grateful for a place where life slows down and tranquility reigns.

In late spring and summer, the quiet beauty of Big Meadows offers travelers a retreat from urban life. *NPS/Mara Meisel*

Rocking chairs and picture windows at Big Meadows Lodge afford the perfect setting from which to enjoy Shenandoah's pastoral beauty. *NPS/John F. Mitchell*

In such a postcard-perfect setting, visitors almost have to pinch themselves to remember that the pastoral beauty of Big Meadows and Shenandoah National Park exists only seventy-five miles or so from the traffic and suburban sprawl of Washington, D.C., and northern Virginia. How that came to be, how a narrow strip of the Blue Ridge Mountains became a sanctuary for harried city-dwellers and road-weary travelers, is a complex story that begins long before people came on the scene. As peaceful as it may appear on a May evening, Shenandoah National Park is a vibrant living entity that has changed dramatically over time. Throughout its seventy-mile length and 3,500-foot range of elevation, the park landscape is the result of forces so powerful and so deliberate that human minds struggle to comprehend them.

MOVABLE EARTH

Standing at an overlook on Skyline Drive or hiking the park's 101-mile stretch of the Appalachian Trail, few things seem more stable than the ground beneath our feet. Yet far below Earth's surface, the landforms of Shenandoah, like those elsewhere on the planet, float on movable tectonic plates. At some point, perhaps about 1.2 billion years ago, a series of collisions between those plates wrinkled

Shenandoah's rocks and mountains may appear stable, but the park landscape is actually the product of long-term geologic change. *NPS*

a portion of the earth's surface into a giant series of mountains known as the Grenville range. Heat and pressure that built up during this Grenville orogeny (the geologists' term for a mountain-building episode) melted and then compressed the giant rocks within the Grenville range. Today those ancient rocks form the basis of the Blue Ridge Mountains in and around Shenandoah.

In its youth, the Grenville range was perhaps comparable to the modern Himalayas, but long before the first primitive life forms emerged in the oceans, millions of years of weathering and erosion reduced the once lofty mountains to little more than a system of rounded hills and valleys. About 570 million years ago, the tectonic plates again shifted, this time separating and allowing lava from deep within the earth to flow out through surface cracks that extended across what is now eastern North America. The lava flows hardened into a thick pile of volcanic rocks. As the earth continued to rift apart, the volcanic rocks slowly subsided to below sea level,

Shenandoah's oldest rocks, like these granitic formations at Hogback Mountain, form the basis of the park's mountain range. *NPS/Eric Butler*

This greenstone cliff at Crescent Rock offers evidence of ancient lava flows that helped create the Shenandoah landscape. *NPS/Eric Butler*

forming a new (geologically speaking) ocean called Iapetus. In that as in all oceans, sediments fell to the bottom to be pressed into hardened rock. Roughly 250 million years ago, following another long period of tectonic movement, the Iapetus Ocean closed as the earth's proto-continents merged into a single land mass called Pangaea. The force of the collisions pushed up the long spine of the Appalachian Mountains that, at the time, towered many thousands of feet above sea level. However, those mountains, too, were destined to the same fate as the Grenville range. Over the next 150 million years the Appalachians eroded into rounded peaks and valleys that took their place in eastern North America when Pangaea separated into the continents recognizable now. Such change continues today, unnoticed by park visitors, as the Atlantic Ocean widens, and tectonic plates slip and grind together in the inexorable movement that is at this moment shaping the Shenandoah of the distant future.

White quartzite formations at Shenandoah's Calvary Rocks were likely first deposited on the floor of an ancient ocean called Iapetus. *NPS/Eric Butler*

Though it takes something of a practiced eye, visitors to the park can still observe the remnants of Shenandoah's geologic past. So-called "basement rocks" that underlie the Blue Ridge can be seen in various formations at Old Rag Mountain, Hogback Mountain, Marys Rock, and Hazel Mountain Overlook. The rocks have a banded appearance, the result of heat and pressure applied to force their components together a billion years ago. Likewise, evidence of the lava flows are visible in the "greenstone" formations at sites such as Stony Man, Crescent Rock, or Indian Run Overlook on Skyline Drive. Some of the sediments from the edge of the Iapetus Ocean are visible in

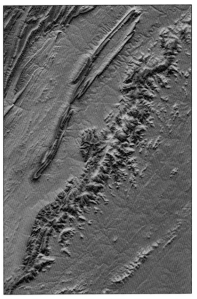

This color-enhanced satellite photograph clearly shows the narrow strip of the Blue Ridge on which Shenandoah National Park rests and the relatively level land on either side. *NASA*

the white quartzite formations at Calvary Rocks. Most of these rocks formed long before terrestrial life on earth. Visitors who search for fossils in Shenandoah will find them mostly in the form of "trace fossils," the burrows left behind by an ancient species of ocean worm. These geologic artifacts, souvenirs from a time humans can scarcely imagine, tell a compelling story of colliding continents and lost oceans that built the very ground on which we walk.

When it comes to park history, geography is as important as geology. Due to complex patterns of uplift and erosion, the Blue Ridge narrows considerably in central and northern Virginia. Indeed, the portion of the Blue Ridge that now comprises Shenandoah National Park is no wider than fifteen miles at any point. This steep and rugged terrain is bounded on the east by the rolling hills of the Virginia Piedmont and on the west by the broad expanse of the Shenandoah Valley. When people, both native and European, came to the region, they would find the lower elevations far more hospitable and view the narrow band of mountains primarily as an obstacle to be crossed on the way to somewhere else.

The same forces that weathered and eroded the ancient Appalachians also gave rise to the rivers and streams of Shenandoah's modern landscape. As the mountains took on their current rounded appearance, groundwater collected in depressed coves high on the mountainsides, feeding underground springs and seeps that sent water spilling down the slopes. Over time, the power of such fast-moving water cut the seventy-odd small watershed basins and ninety small streams visible in the park today. Though they move much slower now than in the geologic past, these are still high-gradient streams, typified by cascades, riffles, waterfalls, and plunge pools.

Today, rain that falls in any of those small park streams and watersheds eventually makes its way into Chesapeake Bay, the nation's largest estuary. The park is thus an important part of the larger Chesapeake Bay watershed that extends north into Pennsylvania and New York. However, due to Shenandoah's unique placement astride the Blue Ridge Mountains, a given raindrop might take any one of several circuitous routes from an Appalachian cove into the Bay.

Imagine a summer rainstorm moving south to north through the park along Skyline Drive. Stalling between Bucks Elbow Mountain and Pasture Fence Mountain, the clouds drop rain on the Wildcat Ridge Parking Area where it works its way down the eastern slope of the Blue Ridge into the headwaters of the Moormans River. The Moormans then flows east and slightly north out of the park, eventually to join the South Fork of the Rivanna River and then the Rivanna River proper. Known as "Mr. Jefferson's River," the Rivanna moves past Charlottesville and into the James River at Columbia, across the fall line near Richmond, and into Chesapeake Bay.

As the storm slips north past Big Meadows, its rain falls on the western slope of the Blue Ridge into the headwaters of Hawksbill Creek, north through the town of Luray, and into the South Fork of the Shenandoah River. The South Fork then meanders north to join the river's North Fork at Front Royal. From there, it flows on to meet the Potomac near Harper's

Shenandoah's coves and valleys give rise to high-gradient small streams that feed three of Virginia's major river systems. *NPS/ Ed Knepley*

Ferry and then southeast to Washington, D.C., and the Chesapeake Bay. A slight shift eastward as the storm moves toward Front Royal, however, could provide a much more direct route to the Bay via the Rappahannock River, across the Piedmont, and into the Bay south of the peninsula known as Virginia's Northern Neck.

The Blue Ridge, then, might be characterized as Shenandoah's continental divide. It shunts water east or west into one of the park's three major river systems—the James, the Shenandoah-Potomac, and the Rappahannock—in much the same fashion, albeit on a much smaller scale, as the Rocky Mountains determine which American rivers flow into the Atlantic and Pacific. The difference in Shenandoah is that the Blue Ridge determines the route, not the destination. Because the park feeds three of the most important river systems in Virginia, what happens in Shenandoah can have profound implications for regions farther east. As isolated as the park might appear from the busy metropolitan areas along the Atlantic coast, millions of residents from Newport News to Washington, D.C., drink water that originates within Shenandoah's boundaries. When it comes to the region's watersheds, what is good for the park is good for all who live downstream.

DISORDERLY ORDER

For a panoramic look at Shenandoah forests, it is hard to beat Jeremys Run Overlook. From this spot, situated at 2,410 feet in elevation on Skyline Drive, motorists can view the steep valley cut by Jeremys Run Creek as it flows west off the Blue Ridge toward the South Fork of the Shenandoah River. Like most of Shenandoah's watersheds, Jeremys Run today is thick with trees that, in summer, cover the valley with a seemingly unbroken canopy of green foliage. Yet however stable the woods might appear on a summer afternoon, the history of these forests is as powerful and complex as that of the mountains and streams below.

Ecologically speaking, Shenandoah's current woodlands are newcomers to the mountain landscape, emerging near the end of the Great Ice Age about 10,000 to 12,000 years ago. The glaciers themselves never made it south to what is now the park, but the cold temperatures associated with the ice sheets encouraged the growth of various spruces, firs, and pines, creating forests like those now visible in southern Canada. Not until the final (so far anyway) glacier began its retreat did the cold-

A view of Shenandoah's forests as seen here from Jeremys Run Overlook, mile 26.4. *NPS/ John F. Mitchell*

adapted trees begin to move farther north and to the highest peaks of the Appalachians. As they moved out, deciduous trees from warmer climes farther south began to migrate north into Shenandoah's coves and valleys.

Apart from human influence, temperature remains an important factor in determining the composition of Shenandoah's forests. These days, however, temperature depends not on retreating glaciers, but on elevation. Generally speaking, each thousand feet of elevation gain brings a corresponding 3-degree Fahrenheit drop in temperature. In the park, elevations range from a mere 591 feet above sea level on the park's extreme northern end to 4,049 feet above sea level at the pinnacle of Hawksbill Mountain. Such variation is especially visible in spring as trees on the lower slopes bud and leaf out first, followed up to a month later by those on the mountain peaks.

In the valleys and on lower slopes where warm weather arrives first and lingers longest, ecologists classify the vegetation as an "oak-hickory" or "Appalachian hardwood" forest. Chestnut oak, white and northern red oak, yellow poplars, and various hickories are among the most prominent trees. Through the nineteenth century, American chestnut also flourished in these woods. Ranging up to a hundred feet tall and twelve feet in diameter, a single American chestnut might shade over forty yards of the forest floor. Before the trees were ravaged by blight in the 1920s and '30s, American chestnuts likely accounted for about 30 percent of the timber in all Shenandoah forests, and in certain areas of the park, that total ran as high as 80 percent. Above 3,000 feet, Appalachian hardwoods slowly give way to what ecologists call the northern hardwood forest, dominated by red maple, yellow birch, and American beech. Various forest shrubs often thrive below the tallest trees creating thick undergrowth. At the highest elevations in Shenandoah, tiny stands of spruce and fir still cling to the mountain ridges as if to remind visitors of the cold-weather vegetation that once dominated the Central Appalachians.

In the nineteenth century, the most prominent trees in Shenandoah's forests were various oaks (bottom) and the American chestnut (top). *NPS/Mara Meisel*

As anyone who hikes one of the park's wooded trails soon discovers, such classifications only hint at the great diversity within Shenandoah's forests. On dry exposed ridges, where moisture runs off quickly, one can find stands of shortleaf and Virginia pines. In cool moist coves and ravines—even at lower elevations, sugar maples, white ash, basswood, and eastern hemlock sometimes flourish. Naturally occurring fires, high winds, and ice storms break or uproot older trees, exposing the forest floor to sunshine and giving rise to pines and other species normally kept out by a lack of light. Fluctuations in animal populations affect the distribution of mast and seed, also an important determinant of forest composition.

A wide variety of wildflowers including wild columbine can be found in Shenandoah's forests. The park has more species of vascular plants than all of Europe. *NPS*

Trees are the most visible, but far from the most numerous plants in Shenandoah forests. Shenandoah has some 1,600 species of vascular plants—more than all of Europe—and trees account for fewer than one hundred of those. Throughout the forests, showy wildflowers such as trillium, wild azaleas, lady slippers, and jack-in-the-pulpit grow alongside an almost infinite variety of ferns and shrubs. Variations in the water table create seeps and springs, giving rise to wetlands and fens like those at Big Meadows that contain grasses and rare plants found nowhere else in the park.

Though it may be difficult to see on a given day, the shady landscapes visitors observe at Jeremys Run and other overlooks—like designs in a kaleidoscope—are constantly shifting to form new patterns on the mountain slopes. Not so long ago, ecologists used the term "climax" to describe mature forests, suggesting that the woods gradually moved from instability in their youth toward maturity and stability in their old age. Today, though, many ecologists discern something more

Shenandoah's rugged terrain and isolated coves helped protect its forests from extensive clear-cutting. *NPS*

complex at work in Appalachian forests. It is best described as a kind of disorderly order. General trends in vegetation patterns can be noted and general labels applied, but the specific form that a Shenandoah forest takes is inevitably a chancy process controlled by variables as unpredictable as a passing storm, a falling tree, or even a busy squirrel. That process, though, proved crucial to the later history of the park. Patchy woods, tucked away into isolated coves or on steep hillsides, would make logging more difficult and less profitable than in other parts of the Appalachians and the confines of Shenandoah would largely be spared from the massive clear-cutting that took place elsewhere.

ANIMALS

Shenandoah's changing forest mosaic has always attracted an astounding variety of wildlife. In the last days of the Ice Age when glaciers held sway over local temperatures, tundra may have been part of the landscape on the highest peaks. If so, it is easy to imagine the incredible array of lemmings, voles, shrews, and mice that populated such habitats as well as the ermine, marten, and other small predators that hunted them. In all likelihood, this near-Arctic environment supported ptarmigans, spruce grouse, caribou, woolly mammoths, mastodons, moose, and musk oxen. Various species of bears and the now-extinct dire wolf might have hunted in what is now Shenandoah. Fossil evidence from other regions suggests that the park was also home to other mammals now long gone from the southern Appalachians and indeed all of North America, including huge ground sloths, giant 300-pound beavers, and long-nosed peccaries.

As the ice sheets slipped northward and temperatures rose, those species that survived retreated to cooler climes. However, modern visitors who seek evidence of Shenandoah's Ice Age past need look no further than the eastern brook trout that now populate park streams and rivers. These beautiful fish with their green backs, orange fins, and delicate red spots outlined in pale blue originated in the northern reaches of the American continent and migrated south with the advancing glaciers. The fish remained in the Central Appalachians only because the shaded mountain streams ran cold and clear enough to support them. Today, aided by conservation efforts and strict fishing regulations, some fifty of the park's ninety smaller streams support vigorous brook trout populations. Smaller fish, including dace, sculpins, chubs, and darters, share the brook trout's cold-water high-elevation habitat. In the lower reaches of park streams, smallmouth bass, perch, and other pan fish draw attention from anglers.

Shenandoah's streams support a vigorous population of eastern brook trout. The fish are holdovers from the park's Ice Age past. *Ann & Rob Simpson*

As hardwood trees replaced tundra and boreal forests in Shenandoah, bird populations boomed. Modern ornithologists have identified more than 200 species of migratory and resident birds in the park, ranging from the common (cardinals, blue jays, eastern towhees, downy woodpeckers, and indigo buntings) to the uncommon (Baltimore ori-

Downy woodpeckers (left) and indigo buntings (right) can be commonly observed in Shenandoah. *Ann & Rob Simpson*

oles, pileated woodpeckers, and great horned owls) to the rare (peregrine falcons, ospreys, and bald eagles). In recent decades, Shenandoah's large swaths of hardwood forests have become especially important to maintaining populations of neotropical birds that depend on the park for summer habitat and as a travel corridor for their migrations to and from the American tropics.

Today the most common mammals in the park are gray squirrels and white-tailed deer. Both have been around since the first humans came into the Blue Ridge, but it is difficult to know with any

Neotropical birds like Baltimore orioles depend on Shenandoah's forests during their seasonal migrations. *Ann & Rob Simpson*

White-tailed deer (left) and eastern gray squirrels (right) are the most common mammals in Shenandoah National Park. *NPS/John F. Mitchell (deer) Ann & Rob Simpson (squirrel)*

certainty how their populations have fluctuated over time. Mast-bearing trees do not always produce bumper crops of acorns and other food to sustain deer. In times past, mountain lions and gray wolves also provided an important population check on the herds. Bobcats, still prevalent in the park, take squirrels and young deer, as well as smaller mammals such as mice and shrews. All the park's mammals move widely in search of food, but when it comes to foraging, few can match the habits of the American black bear. Although they take deer and smaller mammals, especially those weakened by disease or old age, bears are best described as omnivores. They consume a wide range of fish, tree bark, insects, grubs, berries, acorns, and seeds. Some studies suggest that a single black bear may cover some fifteen square miles nightly in its search for food. Current estimates put the park's black bear population somewhere in the hundreds with a given year's number varying according to food supply, severity of weather, natural mortality, and hunting on lands outside the park. Like the forests themselves, mammal populations wax and wane, shift and change, influenced by myriad factors, some obvious, others barely noticeable. From the earliest days of human occupation, the region's abundant wildlife drew hunters

In any given year, Shenandoah is home to several hundred American black bears. *Ann & Rob Simpson*

The rare Shenandoah salamander is the park's only federally designated endangered animal. *NPS/Lester Via*

and trappers out of the surrounding valleys and wildlife populations suffered at their hands. For the most part, though, those who sought meat and skins were a transient crowd who moved on when game became scarce.

America's national parks have devoted much time and energy to studying mammals such as bear and deer because these large animals, the so-called "charismatic megafauna," are the species most appealing to visitors. However, within Shenandoah, as in other parks, large mammals make up a relatively small portion of the overall animal population. Shenandoah is home to twenty-seven species of reptiles, including timber rattlesnakes and painted turtles. Roughly twenty-four species of amphibians inhabit the

Insects like this tiger swallowtail butterfly are among the least studied of the park's animals. *NPS/Ed Knepley*

streams and wetlands, including the rare Shenandoah salamander, the park's only federally designated endangered animal. By far the most numerous and least-studied animals in the park are insects. Some 90,000 species of insects have been identified in the United States. How many of those reside in Shenandoah is anyone's guess, though the park has devoted some study to butterflies (the most attractive), to aquatic insects (important indicators of stream health and food for trout), and to insects classified as pests (especially those that feed on prominent trees).

ELUSIVE NATURE

Visitors from urban areas often think of a trip to Shenandoah as a chance to get back to nature, to a kind of Blue Ridge Eden, a relic preserved from a bygone era, when trees were thick, animals plentiful, and nature balanced and pristine. However, to adopt that view is to miss a fundamental point about the Shenandoah landscape. At no time in the park's past has nature really been pristine or unchanging. Mountains have been pushed up and eroded; streams have cut deeply into watersheds; forests have been subject to the whims of temperature and moisture; and even in the absence of human hunters, animal populations ebb and flow. The change is also ongoing, visible in a passing storm, a flowing stream, or even the banded rocks at the base of an exposed cliff.

However one defines "nature," Shenandoah is a fine place to experience and enjoy it. *NPS*

Acknowledging that "pristine nature" is an elusive concept in no way detracts from an appreciation of Shenandoah. Instead it helps us realize that each visit to the park is unique, an experience exclusive to that particular place and time. More importantly perhaps, it shows how the deep natural history of the region influenced its human history. By the time people arrived, nature had already shaped the area into a narrow, rugged, forested region bounded east and west by more level terrain, characteristics which would prove crucial in its designation as a national park. Finally, a more dynamic view of nature helps us understand that humans are but additional agents of change in an already highly changeable world. With the arrival of people the lives of chestnut trees, brook trout, Shenandoah salamanders, and black bears became entangled with human institutions—families, economies, governments—all of which had at least an equal hand in transforming a slender band of Blue Ridge Mountains into the living park landscape we recognize today.

Chapter II

People are curious beings. Wherever they go, whatever they do, they usually leave something behind. Some of those things, especially if they happen to be fashioned from the ancient rocks of the Blue Ridge Mountains, have remarkable staying power. So it is with the tools used by the first people to see the narrow band of mountains that comprise Shenandoah National Park. Over the years, such tools have been found scattered throughout the park: spear points and knife blades at Lewis Mountain, Tanners Ridge, and Hawksbill, and arrowheads at Big Meadows. Piecing together the lives and life stories of the people who left these items is a bit like trying to reconstruct a house by looking at one or two old bricks, but even such fragmentary evidence can be revealing.

FIRST FOOTPRINTS

Most of the tools left by native people within the confines of the park were implements used in hunting, indicating that native people, those whom we euphemistically call "Indians," came to the Blue Ridge in search of game. And why not? Most evidence suggests that the first humans arrived about 9,000 to 10,000 years ago (maybe as long as

Arrowheads and spear points found in and around Shenandoah offer important clues about the park's first human inhabitants. *NPS/John Amberson*

An atlatl or spear-thrower is a tool that uses leverage to achieve greater velocity in dart-throwing.

13,000 years ago) at a point when the climate was warming with the retreat of the last glaciers. Even if the larger cold-adapted animals—mastodons, musk oxen, woolly mammoths, and moose—had disappeared, the mountains still supported a large population of deer, bear, and smaller game. Hunting them required patience, skill, and most important, constant movement. Indeed, for about 9,000 years, these so-called Archaic people seem to have gone wherever the food supply took them. Traveling in small family-oriented groups, they moved with the seasons. In spring and summer, men likely trapped or speared fish in the rivers while women searched the valleys for wild fruits and edible plants. As the weather cooled in autumn and winter, men moved into the mountains to hunt, perhaps cloaked in deerskins for camouflage. Using a powerful spear-thrower known as an atlatl, a skilled hunter could hit a deer at forty yards and then track the wounded animal through the forest, eventually killing it with a spear driven through its heart. Archaeological studies suggest that small bands of perhaps fifteen to twenty-five people established hunting camps in the Blue Ridge that they visited for two to three months during the year. While men hunted, women likely fanned out into the surrounding forests in search of chestnuts, hickory nuts, and acorns.

Arrowheads found at Big Meadows illustrate an important change in native culture about 3,000 years ago. About then, the Shenandoah region became home to people of the Woodland Tradition, a way of life still in evidence—though in altered form—until the arrival of Europeans. Woodland people in and around Shenandoah traveled in larger groups and, by A.D. 800, hunted with a new weapon: the bow and arrow. Though perhaps no more effective at killing than an atlatl, a bow was easier to carry and arrows could be released quicker and more quietly than spears. Woodland people, too, chose mountain

campsites for hunting, usually setting up temporary dwellings along mountain streams and in level parts of hollows. They might have remained in the mountains longer than their Archaic ancestors, perhaps hunting annually from May to October. It is difficult to know exactly what sorts of animals Woodland people took from Shenandoah forests, but studies done elsewhere in Appalachia show that mountain woods could support a stunning array of game. A ten-square-mile patch of upland forest might contain some 40,000 gray squirrels, 200 wild turkeys, 400 white-tailed deer, a vigorous population of black bears, as well as opossums, rabbits, and raccoons.

Woodland people incorporated hunting into a pattern of seasonal subsistence that included gathering mast and various types of berries. One area that might have proved attractive for food gathering was Big Meadows. Archaeological evidence indicates that native people in the Shenandoah area—like those elsewhere in eastern America—set light ground fires to keep such places open and free of undergrowth. Such fires rarely burned hot enough to affect larger trees, but in consuming briars and woody plants, periodic burns encouraged growth of blueberries that attracted people as well as grasses and browse that drew deer to the area. Some of the most recent archaeological research indicates that Woodland people may have set fires at Big Meadows between October and April, blazes that, along with attracting deer and encouraging useful plants, kept the fields open and easily accessible as a base camp for hunting parties that ventured into the mountains in autumn.

Another change in native culture—one with important implications for the park landscape—occurred sometime shortly after A.D. 800, as people in and around the Blue Ridge began to grow some of their own food. Agriculture likely began with the unintentional cultivation of weeds. Wherever native people went, they constructed dwellings, created fire pits, buried garbage, and generally disturbed the ground around their villages and camps. Especially along the rivers of the adjacent Valley and Piedmont, such turned-up earth attracted weeds and other plants, some of which had edible seeds and leaves. In time, the natives simply began to pull non-useful plants from around those that provided food, creating a kind of chaotic agriculture in the rich soil along the rivers. Gradually, Woodland farmers augmented such "camp followers" with plants such as squash (probably descended from wild gourds) that originated in other areas (in the case of squash, perhaps the Ozarks) and whose seeds accompanied travelers from those regions into Virginia's Piedmont and valleys.

Indians who occupied the level ground adjacent to the Blue Ridge also incorporated corn (or more properly, maize), a crop that originated in Mexico, into their system of agriculture. Easily stored, corn provided good insurance against lean times, but it was not an easy crop to cultivate. Storage of seeds, harvests, and distribution of the surplus were activities that required a measure of new social organization among native people. Farther south in the Tennessee Valley, corn brought about something of a revolution in Indian society with the emergence of large chiefdoms and towns dominated by a single leader. In the valleys of the Blue Ridge, however, growing seasons were shorter and, for the most part, the natives seem to have blended corn into their existing system of hunting, gathering wild foods, and casual agriculture. They planted the grain in hills with squash and beans (another crop from Mexico) so that their gardens or "fields" produced a tangle of food crops. Beans wound around cornstalks, and gourds and squash popped up at odd intervals, a pattern of agriculture that, while it might appear untidy, offered several ecological benefits. Beans helped replace nitrogen taken out of the soil by corn and the dense growth helped control erosion and eliminate competing weeds.

When it comes to park history, the most significant characteristic of agriculture might also be its most obvious. However it is practiced, farming is best suited to level ground. As a result, the Indian people who occupied the area around Shenandoah came to favor the adjacent valleys for villages and agricultural fields. Generally speaking, they lived there and fanned out onto the slopes of the mountains in search of game and wild foods. By the time the first Europeans arrived in Virginia, the Piedmont was home to well-established native groups known to whites as Monocans and Manahoacs. We are less certain about the Shenandoah Valley because conflicts between native groups and diseases introduced by European traders had reduced Indian populations there before English settlers arrived. However, the word "Shenandoah" is perhaps an English corruption of a Native American term. Today, the most popular and romanticized Indian meaning attached to Shenandoah is "valley of the stars." What we can be sure of, though, is that the Blue Ridge, even during its earliest stages of human occupation, remained important for its resources, but the milder Valley and Piedmont proved more attractive for settlement.

From our modern perspective, this native world—Shenandoah before the "white man"—is easily misunderstood. Too often, we picture Indians as children of nature, having little impact on the land and living a life of perpetual abundance. However, if we could somehow step back into the fifteenth century, before the arrival of Europeans in Virginia, it would be easy to note the human presence around Shenandoah. Tangled gardens and cornfields, fire-maintained hunting areas, a labyrinth of trails, valley villages, and well-defined hunting and fishing territories would offer clear evidence that native people took full advantage of Blue Ridge resources. Moreover, life was not always easy. A spring drought, an early fall frost, a shortfall of acorns and hickory nuts, a slight downturn in the deer population—any of these might force Indians to alter their seasonal subsistence patterns. Sporadic hunger and occasionally serious food shortages were problems that Shenandoah natives, like all humans, constantly had to solve.

In general terms, however, two factors distinguished native land use from that of the whites who would follow. First, native populations in the region remained relatively low, apparently numbering in the low thousands at the time of European contact. Local shortages of food or other items could frequently be remedied simply by moving to another locale. Second, although Indians understood what we would call the concept of private property, they were not part of a capitalistic market economy. Nor did they dedicate themselves to the unrestricted accumulation of goods. Indians living in the Valley or Piedmont might offer deerskins or corn to other natives as an indication of their desire for friendship and peaceful relations. Those receiving the "gift" were then obligated to respond in kind either immediately or at some later date. Thus, within the native economy, deerskins and corn were valuable primarily for what they could provide—clothing and food—not as abstract "products" with values dictated by a distant market. Generosity, the ability to give away lots of goods (and thereby acquire obligations and loyalty), was the goal of nearly every Indian chieftain so that personal relationships, not prices, were the determining factors in trade within and among the natives. That changed with the arrival of European explorers and colonists.

COMMODITIES

For well over a half-century following the settlement of Jamestown, the Virginia upcountry remained terra incognita, at least as far as most English colonists were concerned. In 1669–1670, accompanied by several Indian guides, a German explorer named John Lederer sent back the first written reports of the Piedmont and mountains. Much of Lederer's account is pure fantasy (he reported giant brackish lakes and vast expanses of sandy desert that required a fortnight to cross), but most historians believe that he climbed the eastern side of the Blue Ridge and glimpsed the Shenandoah Valley from some point in what is now the park, perhaps Hawksbill or High Top.

During the last decades of the seventeenth century, the Virginia colony secured its western borders and established a series of forts along the fall lines of the colony's major rivers. From those forts, explorers began to move into the backcountry, hoping to establish trade relations with Indians beyond the Blue Ridge. By 1716, the search for new land to accommodate a slowly expanding Virginia population brought the colony's royal governor, Alexander Spotswood, to the crest of the Blue Ridge. Spotswood likely passed through what is now the park, perhaps at Swift Run Gap or at Milam Gap. Fifteen years later, a handful of English colonists had settled in the Shenandoah Valley. As tales of the flat fertile farmland spread, more settlers followed, following trails across the Blue Ridge or journeying south down the Valley from Maryland and Pennsylvania.

European settlement of the Virginia Piedmont and Shenandoah Valley forever changed economics and ecology in the region surrounding the park. *NPS/John Amberson*

English settlement brought with it an ecological transformation. Old World diseases such as smallpox, measles, and influenza devastated local Indian populations, forcing natives who escaped the contagions to move or form new societies and alliances. European livestock grazed indigenous grasses into extinction to be replaced by Old World species more adapted to continuous cropping by domesticated animals. Single-crop fields of tobacco, corn, wheat, and other grains replaced tangled Indian food plots. More importantly, though, English settlers brought with them a new way of understanding the exchange of goods. Nearly everything that could be acquired in the forests or harvested from colonial farms had value beyond its immediate local use. Any product English people could produce in quantity could be sold; what had been resources for Indians became commodities for colonists.

That new relationship did not bode well for the region's wildlife. By the early 1700s, cowhides were in short supply in England due to a series of deadly bovine epidemics that afflicted European cattle. As a result, English leatherworkers turned to American deerskins for making gloves, saddles, book bindings, and harnesses. By 1750, yellow deerskin breeches or buckskins, once the clothing of poor laborers, became a fashion fad among the English upper classes. The first English traders into the Blue Ridge found the Indians more than willing to exchange deerskins (which the natives regarded as common items) for exotic metal pots, hatchets, knives, and ornamental goods.

To protect their cattle and other livestock, European colonists and their descendents virtually eliminated wolves and other predators from the Shenandoah region. *NPS Archives*

Later, guns and liquor also became staples of the Indian trade, items that quickly increased native dependency on European suppliers. As Indians and European settlers began to provide leather for the English market, white-tailed deer populations began to decline. Something on the order of a million deerskins were shipped out of Virginia between 1698 and 1715. Hundreds of thousands more went overland to ports in the Carolinas.

Game laws designed to curb reckless colonial hunting tell a story of growing scarcity. Virginia imposed its first closed hunting season in 1699, restrictions that were renewed and refined throughout the 1700s. By 1772, the colony found it necessary to impose a four-year-moratorium on the killing of any wild deer. Deer apparently never became extinct in the Blue Ridge, in part because English settlers also employed laws to combat predators that threatened livestock as well as deer. Virginia routinely offered bounties on wolves' heads, instructing county clerks to remove the ears from each head they received, lest some wily hunter attempt to turn in the same head twice. The colonial government also encouraged extermination of mountain lions and black bears (which had the annoying habit of attacking settlers' pigs). Virginia even offered colonists payment for crows' heads and "squirrels' scalps" to limit depredations on corn and other crops. By 1800, within a century of English settlement of the Piedmont and Valley, market hunting for skins and the wholesale elimination of pests and predators had drastically altered the region's wildlife population.

Among the older objects in the Shenandoah National Park Archives is a strange-looking hand tool called a "bark spud." Forged of iron, it is essentially a metal rod, with a hand loop at one end and a flattened tip. One might wonder about its purpose were it not for another document housed in the archives, a hand-written "Memorandum of Agreement" dated March 22, 1886. The agreement is,

A bark spud was used to remove bark from felled timber. *NPS Archives*

in effect, a contract, obligating one Isaac Somers to deliver fifty tons of "chestnut oak bark" in "good Merchantable condition" to John H. Sherman, owner of a tannery in Luray, Virginia. The price for the bark: six dollars per ton.

Together, these two artifacts tell us much about the ecological and economic relationships between the Blue Ridge and the Valley during the nineteenth century. Bark from chestnut oaks, American chestnuts, hemlocks, and white oaks (pried from the trees with a bark spud) could be boiled and processed to extract tannin, a substance crucial to processing and preserving leather. All those trees, however, are most prominent at higher elevations. Any Valley tanner who needed such material had to hire a woodsman to venture up the slopes of the Blue Ridge, harvest the bark, and then transport it to his tannery, where it was collected, boiled, and the valuable substance extracted. Much like native people before them, nineteenth-century Virginians viewed the narrow slip of the Blue Ridge as a storehouse of resources, though with one crucial difference: those resources could now be sold on the open market.

Harvesting tree bark was only one of many economic opportunities afforded by Blue Ridge forests. The most valuable commodity was the hardwood timber itself. Local sawmill owners cut chestnut, oak, maple, poplar, and a host of other trees into lumber for construction.

Hauling and harvesting tree bark, from which Valley leatherworkers extracted tannin, was an important activity in and around the Blue Ridge. *Shenandoah County Historical Society*

Residents relied on the Blue Ridge forests for nearly all their wooden needs, including wagons, tool handles, mill wheels, shingles, brooms, and a wide variety of other items.

Timber was also the region's most valuable fuel. With roads and turnpikes now crossing the Blue Ridge at every major gap, firewood cut from the slopes became crucial to the winter comfort of Valley and Piedmont settlers. Wood, or more properly charcoal, produced by burning wood, fueled Virginia's iron industry, making the state a leading producer of that metal throughout the first half of the nineteenth century. To extract the metal from its rock, smelters built large stone furnaces in the mountain forests, often surrounded by barracks that could house and feed up to a hundred men. The crews cut timber from the surrounding woods and burned it into charcoal that, in turn, provided heat for the extraction process. Some estimates suggest that a single iron furnace required about nineteen cords of wood for every twenty-four hours of operation. In a year, a single furnace operation might clear 1,700 to 1,800 acres of hardwood.

The remains of an iron furnace. Iron extraction, which used timber for fuel, led iron-producers to clear small tracts of Blue Ridge forest. *NPS*

John A. Alexander owned one such operation on Madison Run. Between 1865 and 1879, Alexander's operation completely denuded the slopes around the furnace. As was typical of most such proprietors, Alexander shut the furnace down when it became too expensive to transport wood from more distant tracts. Alexander's operation was typical in another way: he appears to have been an absentee landowner. In summer, farmers from the Piedmont and Valley routinely drove their cattle to mountain pastures, including those at Big Meadows that were still maintained with periodic fires set by the herders. The cooler climate was also well suited to apple orchards, at first attended by absentee owners who showed up in late summer to harvest the fruit.

By century's end, railroads had made their way into the Appalachians. A line crossed Rockfish Gap and ran through the Valley to Front Royal in 1880. Because they provided easy transport of timber products to distant markets, railroads had the potential to increase exploitation of the Blue Ridge forests. Indeed, that is precisely what happened south of Shenandoah in western North Carolina, where northern lumber companies built rail lines onto even the highest slopes and quickly cleared whole mountainsides of timber. Though similar operations could be found in some of Virginia's mountain forests, geography protected lands that would become Shenandoah National Park from extensive railroad logging. The steep narrow band of mountains simply contained too little easily accessible timber to make such an enterprise economically feasible. Moreover, elevations were lower than in the southern Appalachians, meaning that some of the most valuable trees, such as red spruce and Fraser fir, did not form the vast unbroken forests that attracted lumber barons to other parts of Appalachia.

HIGH PLACES AND HOLLOWS

By the late nineteenth century, Virginians settling in the Blue Ridge discovered another marketable commodity: cool summers. Living in modern America where we take air conditioning for granted, it is difficult to appreciate just how trying a southern summer—say, in Charleston, Wilmington, or Norfolk—could be. To escape the heat and the outbreak of malaria that often followed, coastal plain residents of sufficient means sought respite in the Appalachians. Virginia's Blue Ridge entrepreneurs began to cater to such folk at an early date, establishing hotels first at Blackrock Springs and later at Skyland, located near the highest point in today's park. In time, both establishments

The remains of farm implements found around Shenandoah's old homesteads help tell the story of rural life in the Blue Ridge. *NPS/John F. Mitchell*

developed into resorts modeled on those of the Catskills, with hiking trails, horseback riding, swimming, and fishing. Guests from warmer climes stayed in rustic cabins and, at Skyland, ate in a large dining hall with a sprawling view of the Shenandoah Valley. By the 1920s, Skyland attracted hundreds of such guests every summer.

Farther down the ridges, in the hollows and narrow bottomlands along major streams, other people moved in. Weakley Hollow, between Old Rag or Ragged Mountain and the Blue Ridge proper, attracted settlers in the 1770s. A site in Nicholson Hollow along Hughes River appears to have been settled in the 1790s. Life there seems to have been profitable due to the fertile soils of the river bottomland. Like farmers in the Valley, those in Nicholson Hollow sold surplus crops at regional markets and invested in slaves. Remains of a slave cabin discovered there date from the 1820s. The Weakley Hollow settlement eventually became the town of Old Rag, which, by the 1920s, had its own post office, stores, churches, and school.

The most extensive settlement, however, came in the decades after the Civil War. Together with agriculture and forest industries such as lumbering and bark collection, service jobs at the resorts and the opportunity to sell crafts and produce to seasonal residents led to a varied way of life for most mountain people. Local color writers and sociologists who traveled in the region in the 1930s often stereotyped these Blue Ridge residents as poor, primitive, uneducated, and isolated from urban America. However, much like Native Americans, these Shenandoah people left behind trappings of their culture that tell a different story.

Excavating old home sites, archaeologists have found patent medicine bottles, ceramics, phonograph records, and mechanical toys—perhaps purchased by way of the Sears, Roebuck catalog—all of which suggest that the majority of mountain folk were fully integrated into America's emerging consumer culture. Moreover, the discovery of automobile parts around old homesteads indicates that mountain people had both the means and inclination to venture well beyond the confines of their farms. Isolated pockets of poverty existed in Shenandoah—as in other parts of Appalachia—but the so-called "poor mountaineer" is now largely regarded as a misleading stereotype created by outsiders. Estimates vary, but at least 450 families still lived in what was to become Shenandoah National Park in 1935, making their living from the land and seasonal visitors, spending extra money on luxuries, traveling to nearby towns, and generally living like rural folk in other parts of America.

Dish fragments, soft drink bottles, a medicine bottle, and even a child's toy ray gun—all recovered from archaeological digs around Shenandoah homesteads—suggest that, by the early twentieth century, mountain people were fully integrated into America's emerging consumer culture. *NPS Archives*

"NATURE" ON THE EVE OF THE PARK

Without question, white settlement in the Blue Ridge changed the Shenandoah landscape. Removal of trees for lumber, charcoal, and tannin extract left large sections of the forest floor exposed to the drying effects of the sun. Cutover tracts became much more susceptible to wildfire and, once burned, suffered from heavy erosion during spring rains. Comparatively speaking, though, the narrow ridge that would become Shenandoah National Park was in better shape than much of the surrounding area. Across eastern America, nearly all of the original forest cover had been removed to accommodate settlement and industry.

Estimates done in the 1940s indicate that, on average, less than 1 percent of old-growth forest remained intact east of the Mississippi River.

Even so, a systematic study of Shenandoah's forests conducted in the 1930s suggests that most of its woodlands were in relatively good shape. Only about 14.5 percent of lands proposed for the park remained completely clear of timber and most of the open tracts had been used for crops and pasturelands. Only four of the park's seventy-odd watersheds showed evidence of severe erosion. Though nearly all the park's watersheds exhibited signs of past logging (mostly by absentee landowners) and periodic fires, those who conducted the study found little evidence of extensive clear-cutting. Instead, they noted that although some species—American chestnut, chestnut oak, and various hardwoods used for fuel—had been "reduced" by commercial operations, most areas generally showed "good tree growth." Certain forests on Overall Run were exceptions; the timber there was accessible and the region had been devastated by wildfire between 1930 and 1934. Nature's restocking process, as always, seemed chaotic, frequently mixing pines and hardwoods in odd ways that taxed 1930s schemes of forest classification. Like the rest of eastern America, Shenandoah also had

This photograph, taken from the summit of Old Rag Mountain in 1916, suggests that the region that became the park remained relatively free of clear-cuts and extensive logging. *NPS Archives*

View from Timber Hollow Overlook (mile 43.3), 1936, showing the forested ridges of
Shenandoah with cleared land in the valley below. *NPS Archives*

scattered stands of virgin timber. Indeed, some estimates put remaining
old growth as high as 30 percent of the total forested landscape. By almost any measure, Shenandoah was not a worn-out landscape. In contrast to the Valley and the Virginia Piedmont, future parkland boasted a
vigorous growth of flourishing woodlands pleasing to the eye.

Many modern visitors think of national parks, particularly those in
the East, as rescuing and preserving scenic regions from the ravages
of civilization and commercialism. The establishment of Great Smoky
Mountains National Park, for example, put an end to lumbering in
the region and preserved what was left of the area's ancient forests.
Mammoth Cave National Park probably saved a natural wonder from
becoming another tacky roadside tourist attraction. Shenandoah's
early history defies such a simplistic narrative. In fact, it is far more
likely that when Congress began to search for eastern park sites in the
1920s, Shenandoah drew attention precisely because the region had
not yet been devastated by industrial logging or abusive commercial
agriculture. Likewise, the tourist trade had been restricted to regions
such as Skyland. Other areas of the proposed park had not developed
extensive roads and the accompanying infrastructure of accommodations, restaurants, and souvenir stands that usually sprang up around
prominent attractions. A narrow strip of the Blue Ridge that had, for
millennia, been used primarily by people who lived elsewhere seemed
a perfect locale for a national park. Only one problem remained: how
should the landscape be managed to accommodate the thousands of
tourists now certain to visit?

Chapter III

VISIONS OF WILDERNESS

Many visitors to national parks come to escape the trappings of modern society, to interact—however briefly and from however great a distance—with the American wilderness. Wilderness, though, is a term almost as difficult to define as nature itself. As historian Roderick Nash writes, "wilderness" is a "noun that acts like an adjective." It "produces a certain mood or feeling in a given individual" so that no two people are likely to think of wilderness in the same way. Put more succinctly, "One man's wilderness may be another's roadside picnic ground."

Moreover, "wilderness" cannot exist apart from its cultural counterpart: "civilization." In Shenandoah or anywhere else, one cannot imagine wilderness without also imagining civilization and vice versa. It should come as no surprise then that the trappings of modern urban life played a large role in defining the park's wilderness. Chief among those transforming agents was a machine synonymous with urban life, one that at first might appear to be the direct antithesis of anything wild: the automobile.

"LANDSCAPED WILDERNESS"

In its first report that recommended establishment of Shenandoah National Park in 1924, the Southern Appalachian National Park Committee proposed "a possible skyline drive along the mountain top." The committee had done its homework. Although cars had been around since the 1890s, two recent innovations in automobile technology had made the vehicles more widely available and more reliable. Henry Ford's use of the assembly line and interchangeable parts had drastically reduced production costs. In addition, General Motors engineer Thomas Midgley had discovered that adding lead to gasoline (to produce so-called "ethyl") stopped engine knock and vastly improved performance. By the time serious discussion of Skyline Drive began, nearly 50 percent of Americans owned cars and automobile touring was rapidly becoming a national obsession. With 40,000,000 potential visitors within a day's

Planning for Skyline Drive (shown here) began well before Congress approved Shenandoah National Park. *NPS/John F. Mitchell*

drive of the proposed park, accommodating thousands of auto tourists simply made sense. But this would not be just another highway. As the committee carefully noted, it would provide motorists with sweeping dramatic views of both the Shenandoah Valley and the Virginia Piedmont. "Few scenic drives in the world could surpass it."

Skyline Drive boosters also got an assist from President Herbert Hoover. In 1928, the president built a summer fishing camp on the Rapidan River. With Hoover's backing and his insistence that the road be built using local labor and a modicum of federal money, construction began on Skyline Drive in 1931. The park was still four years in the future, but the road had a one-hundred-foot right-of-way and the support of most local residents who viewed it as an economic boon to the region.

The deepening Great Depression and the election of Franklin Delano Roosevelt in 1932 had important implications for Skyline Drive. Within thirty-seven days of Roosevelt's inauguration in 1933, the Civilian Conservation Corps (CCC) enlisted its first recruits. Roughly one month later, the first CCC workers arrived at Skyland and Big Meadows, providing an additional source of labor for Skyline Drive. In December 1935, final approval for Shenandoah National Park afforded a much wider

Construction of Skyline Drive required extensive excavation and earth movement. *NPS Archives*

Overlooks along Skyline Drive required buttressing with rocks or timber. *NPS Archives*

right-of-way for the road, at last allowing for the scenic drive originally envisioned by the committee.

Whatever the setting, road construction nearly always takes a toll on the natural environment. That was especially true of Skyline Drive because the route across the crest of the Blue Ridge required massive excavation. In the early phases of construction, before establishment of the park, the narrow right-of-way required clearing steep slopes on either side of the roadbed, leaving them open to erosion from spring rains. Indeed, more erosion resulted from construction of Skyline Drive than from all the agricultural and logging activities of the previous decades. In addition, the roadbed required huge amounts of crushed stone and thousands of logs for buttressing, extracted mostly from local sources.

After 1935, wider rights-of-way that came with the park and the continuing availability of CCC labor allowed for better construction practices. Under the watchful eye of chief landscape architect Harvey

Guard rails and overlook walls constructed of native stone gave the Skyline Drive a more finished look. *NPS Archives*

Benson, crews began to smooth out the roadside's steepest slopes. They built overlooks and cut away trees to provide passing motorists with suitable views. Log rails, stone walls, and stone gutters provided more safety and gave the roadway a finished look.

Perhaps most importantly, CCC crews replanted graded and eroded roadsides with various trees and shrubs. Most of the plants were native to Shenandoah or hybrids of native species brought to Skyline Drive from various commercial nurseries and other areas of the park. All told, the CCC planted some 300,000 trees along Skyline Drive. Reed Engle, the park's premiere historian of the CCC, noted, "These efforts were all part of Benson's careful creation of 'natural' vistas and varied topographic features along the length of the Drive." In truth, though, Engle explains, "no area within immediate view of the Skyline Drive in fact is natural," but rather the direct result of systematic planning and landscaping.

Other amenities followed. Campgrounds, restrooms ("comfort stations" in park parlance), picnic grounds, and hiking trails allowed motorists limited access to areas adjacent to Skyline Drive. Skyland Resort, renovated and refurbished several times to keep up with increased tourism, continued to draw its share of visitors. Perhaps the crown jewel of the Skyline Drive is Big Meadows Lodge, constructed from native stone (acquired from Massanutten Mountain) in 1939. Much like Skyline Drive itself, the lodge's great room affords visitors the chance to observe nature from the comfort of a rocking chair. To supply water to such facilities, the CCC changed the course of mountain springs and built large reservoirs, again re-working the landscape for the benefit of auto tourists.

Visitors throughout the years have enjoyed Big Meadows Lodge's great room. The lodge was constructed in 1939. *VA State Chamber of Commerce staff photo/Flournoy*

CCC crews helped create the "windshield wilderness," replanting native species along Skyline Drive. *NPS Archives*

The ideas of Harlan Kelsey, a botanist, landscape architect, and member of the committee that recommended Shenandoah as a national park, provide the best example of the complex (and sometimes contradictory) thinking that went into planning the vistas and attractions along Skyline Drive. Kelsey, who was also president of the Appalachian Trail Conference, first opposed the road because of its potential impact on the trail. Once the park was established with Skyline Drive as a major attraction, though, Kelsey argued for a constructed landscape that would restore the region's plant communities "as they originally existed." However, after driving the new road, even Kelsey had to admit that the view was at times "monotonous." He soon came to favor several ideas from Frederick Law Olmsted, America's premiere landscape architect, to provide a more varied visual experience for drivers. Kelsey pushed for even more overlooks with unobstructed views of the Shenandoah Valley and Piedmont. Elsewhere, he believed, the vegetation should appear to grow outward from the road, with favored perennials and shrubs such as azaleas nearest the roadside and taller trees, especially hardwoods, nearer the bordering forest. Such planting schemes suggested that the "civilization" of the roadway quickly gave way to the "wilderness" of Shenandoah's forests.

Understanding that Skyline Drive offers drivers scenery and lodging planned by landscape architects should not detract from enjoyment of the road and the services it offers visitors. Indeed, in some ways, providing what national park historian David Louder describes as "windshield wilderness" indicates a highly sophisticated understanding of both people and nature. In planning for the needs of drivers, the architects and the CCC workers were, in fact, creating a place for auto tourists on the park landscape—a place that they believed would allow visitors to experience nature without intruding excessively upon it. Correcting problems of early road construction and replanting with native species might also be considered a form of ecological restoration, a way to manipulate the landscape to make it more closely resemble visitors' notions of wilderness, to make it, in a sense, more wild. That so many people today drive the road and enjoy the views without ever recognizing that the setting is "man-made" is perhaps the best testament to the success of those who planned and built it. As Lou Henry Hoover, wife of the president who first backed Skyline Drive, put it, the scenic roadway was (and is) "a splendid work of natural art."

Landscaped wilderness. Today motorists on Skyline Drive get the sense that the civilization of the highway gives way to the wilderness of the surrounding forests. *NPS/John F. Mitchell*

For tourists cruising Skyline Drive, Shenandoah's forests were the most important part of the scenery and park officials quickly set about remaking the woods in the image of wilderness. The transformation began with the elimination of people from the park's forests. By the late 1930s, removal and resettlement of those who once lived on park land had depleted Shenandoah of all but a handful of permanent human inhabitants. Whatever one thinks of the politics and morality of removal, the ecological implications of the policy were profound: For the first time since the end of the Ice Age, no one hunted or farmed the Blue Ridge landscape. With people gone, fields and gardens became ragged weedy grasslands; trees from nearby forests invaded pastures and orchards; homes and farm buildings fell into disrepair.

With the removal of permanent human inhabitants from the park, old agricultural fields like this one began to grow up into forests. *Library of Congress*

Park planners like Harlan Kelsey, however, did not believe in simply letting nature take its course. Much like the vistas along Skyline Drive, park forests might be manipulated and improved by careful management. Almost immediately, work crews began cleaning up and burning brush around former farmsteads. By 1938, the CCC had an elaborate plan to restore the region's "original forest growth." The plan relied heavily on the ideas of pioneer ecologist Frederic Clements, who believed that woodlands moved from instability in their youth to the equilibrium of a "climax forest" in their old age. All the CCC had to do, Kelsey suggested, was simply replant various climax communities in the appropriate locales within the park.

Ultimately, however, Kelsey's scheme proved too ambitious even for the most dedicated Shenandoah planners. Though workers planted some formerly brushy plots with so-called desirable trees—black locust, Fraser fir, and black walnut—they used most of their nursery stock for the landscaping along Skyline Drive. In addition, planners discovered

View from Jewell Hollow Overlook, 1950. By the 1950s, Shenandoah's forests were rapidly covering formerly cleared areas. *NPS Archives*

that in simplifying forest patterns by planting a single species, they invited invasions from indigenous insects and fungi. As a result, more manpower had to be devoted to combating pests like locust leafminers and white pine blister rust. By the early 1940s, when World War II depleted the CCC workforce, the park's forests were a curious mixture of nature's chaotic measures and the systematic work of the CCC.

A Blue Ridge landscape largely devoid of permanent human residents had important implications for wildlife populations. With neither natural predators nor human hunters to cull their numbers, gray squirrels returned in abundance. Other species got help from park officials. Wildlife experts released white-tailed deer, wild turkeys, and a pair of beavers in the park during the 1930s. When a local man shot the male beaver, park officials had him arrested and he spent three weeks in jail, an indication of just how seriously park officials took the reintroduction of wildlife. Fish, too, got an assist from those interested in restoring Shenandoah's wilderness. During the last years of the 1930s, CCC workers and state game officials stocked some 50,000 trout in Shenandoah streams, especially important since visitors could fish (but not hunt) in the new national park.

Removing people as permanent residents on the landscape dramatically affected another element that had shaped the landscape since the end of the Ice Age: fire. For thousands of years, Indians and, to a lesser

Fire towers like this one built by the CCC were part of a general policy of fire suppression at Shenandoah during the 1930s and 1940s. *NPS Archives*

extent, perhaps white settlers, had used fire to maintain cleared or semi-cleared areas for agriculture and hunting. Now, however, as park officials embraced the conservationist mantra of the 1930s, fire, both natural and man-made, became the enemy. During dry seasons, CCC crews stood ready at a moment's notice to deploy into the woods to combat every blaze. Park officials also dispatched crews to clean out undergrowth and "duff" from forest areas that seemed especially prone to fire. At the most dangerous seasons, park employees manned towers set up at select locations, ever watchful for signs of smoke.

Statistics kept by park staff show that the number of fires in Shenandoah declined by 50 percent between 1936 and 1941. Fire suppression eventually proved something of a double-edged sword. On the positive side, CCC crews could and did combat wildfires that might have destroyed hundreds of acres of woodlands. However, without natural or controlled human-set fires to suppress new tree growth, open spaces in forests soon closed. Shenandoah employees had to maintain scenic meadows and grasslands by mowing or by prescribed burning, thereby using park policy to achieve results once obtained by interaction of the human inhabitants with nature.

Efforts to reconstruct Blue Ridge forests underscore just how problematic the term "wilderness" can be when applied to Shenandoah National Park. If one defines "wilderness" as nature on its own, devoid of people, then Shenandoah, in fact, had never fit that bill, at least not since the end of the Ice Age. Moreover, as Justin Reich, a careful student of park policy, explains, efforts to bring back wilderness on this narrow strip of the Blue Ridge—whether they involved replanting forests, restocking wildlife, or fire suppression—required considerable planning and human intervention. According to Reich, instead

President Franklin Delano Roosevelt summed up Shenandoah's purpose well at the park dedication when he noted that it was for both recreation and re-creation of the natural world. *NPS Archives*

of thinking about the national park as preserving wilderness, it is far more accurate to envision the creation of Shenandoah as swapping one human management scheme for another.

That point does not seem to have been lost on Franklin Delano Roosevelt. In his speech dedicating Shenandoah National Park, the president noted, "The creation of this park is one part of our great program of husbandry—the joint husbandry of our human resources and our natural resources." The park, the president perceptively noted, was dedicated to "succeeding generations of Americans for the recreation and the re-creation of what we shall find there." Considering that the park today provides amenities for tourists while at the same time protecting its forested landscape, it would be difficult to find a better description of what Shenandoah was and is.

A WILDERNESS TRAIL

One person who never questioned the benefits of wilderness was a Harvard-educated, free-thinking forester named Benton MacKaye (pronounced to rhyme with "rye"). Finding U.S. Forest Service policies oriented too much toward management for logging and other commercial enterprises, MacKaye argued that what most twentieth-century Americans really needed was time outdoors to renew their vigor and their optimism. Without an appropriate wilderness

Benton MacKaye: promoter of wilderness and founder of the Appalachian Trail Conference. *Appalachian Trail Conference*

escape, MacKaye insisted, urban Americans were as "potentially helpless as canaries in a cage." After leaving the Forest Service, MacKaye in 1921 proposed what he called a "project in regional planning," namely a series of wilderness communities or work camps in the Appalachian Mountains connected by a footpath that spanned the range from New England to the South. The communities, MacKaye believed, would provide sites to which Americans could go and work outdoors. In the process, they could restore both the land and their spirits. In 1925, MacKaye organized an Appalachian Trail Conference in Washington, D.C. Attendees included foresters, hikers, and other wilderness aficionados. They formed a new organization (also known as the Appalachian Trail Conference) in hopes of creating a 2,000-mile path through the woods, now known as the Appalachian National Scenic Trail (AT).

A dedicated corps of hiking enthusiasts worked tirelessly to refurbish existing trails, construct new paths, and then mark and connect them all. In Virginia's Blue Ridge Mountains, that task fell to the Potomac Appalachian Trail Club (PATC). Many members of the club were also regular visitors to Skyland. By 1931 (well before the establishment of the park and before completion of the entire AT in 1937), the PATC had constructed a trail across the crest of the mountains that, not coincidentally, ran right through the resort.

Myron Avery, president of the Potomac Appalachian Trail Club (right) with Benton MacKaye. Avery worked to find a suitable route for the Appalachian Trail through Shenandoah. *Appalachian Trail Conference*

Unfortunately, the route put MacKaye and wilderness advocates on a collision course with supporters of Skyline Drive, who insisted that the best location for the new road was essentially right on top of the trail. Caught in the middle was PATC president Myron Avery. He favored the proposal for Shenandoah National Park because it would protect the land around the trail. However, there would likely be no park without Skyline Drive. After considering the problem, Avery and the PATC came to believe that the new road did not necessarily threaten hikers. The trail could be relocated farther down slope and situated on the rim of the Blue Ridge escarpment—a compromise eventually accepted by the club and the park. Even so, construction of the Skyline Drive and a contemporary proposal to construct a similar road across the peaks of the Great Smokies led to a falling out between MacKaye and the PATC. Suspicious of automobiles and the access they provided to wilderness, MacKaye eventually left the national ATC and became a founding member of the Wilderness Society. It was not the last time that two competing visions of wilderness would have to be accommodated in Shenandoah.

Once the decision to move the trail had been made, the CCC went to work cutting a new path through the Shenandoah woods, complete with trail shelters and other amenities for hikers. According to contemporary accounts, the new route was, in some ways, better suited to hiking than the previous trek through Skyland. In 1937, two members of the PATC noted that "one striking contrast" between the old and new trails was "the absence of views along the old and the constant succession of breath-taking panoramas from the new route." The relocation, the hikers believed, offered the perfect combination of "paramount scenic attractions with a complete sense of isolationism." In addition,

Before and after Appalachian Trail construction at Marys Rock, a popular destination for hikers. *NPS Archives*

Skyline Drive and the access it offered made it possible "to spend every weekend for two years on overnight walking trips in the park and never duplicate the territory covered."

Though the Shenandoah landscape has changed since the late 1930s, and the route of the AT has been shifted to accommodate the idiosyncrasies of both people and nature, the 101-mile stretch of the trail in the park still reflects the compromises made early in its history. The PATC and the National Park Service share maintenance and administration of the trail. Serious backcountry enthusiasts and thru-hikers of the AT can spend days or weeks on the Shenandoah section of the trail. Likewise, those who seek something less rigorous can drive to within easy reach of a trailhead or connecting path and embark on day-hikes ranging from a few minutes to twelve-hour excursions. It may not be exactly what Benton MacKaye envisioned in the 1920s—neither it nor the rest of the AT have the sort of wilderness work camps he advo-

Today hikers enjoy some 101 miles of the Appalachian Trail in Shenandoah National Park. *NPS/John F. Mitchell (hiker) NPS (post)*

cated—but it does afford a large segment of today's urban and suburban Americans a measure of escape into the natural world. Ironically, their ability to escape their "cages" has been aided by the automobiles MacKaye so distrusted.

LEGAL WILDERNESS

On September 3, 1964, the United States did something no nation had ever done. Following a nearly unanimous vote in Congress, President Lyndon Johnson signed into law a remarkable piece of legislation known as the Wilderness Act. Simply stated, the Wilderness Act preserves and protects lands "in their natural condition... without permanent improvement or human habitation." Taking a stab at defining the indefinable, the act describes wilderness as "an area of earth and its community untrammeled by man, where man himself is a visitor who does not remain." In keeping with the paradoxical relationship between automobiles and wilderness, such areas were to be "roadless," open only to travel on foot or horseback.

In its final form, the Wilderness Act represented decades of hard work and lobbying by those who believed that wild places benefited the human spirit. Many of the bill's advocates had been associated with the Wilderness Society, the same organization that Benton MacKaye helped found in the 1930s. The bill's chief author and architect, Howard Zahniser, was a former president of the Society. Zahniser's use of "untrammeled" to describe wilderness struck some observers as odd, but in this context, the word means unfettered or unrestrained. Simply stated, the Wilderness Act set certain lands free from people, allowing the regions to be whatever they might become under nature's influence. As part of the search for lands to liberate, the secretary of the interior required every national park to review all roadless areas of more than 5,000 acres and assess their potential as wilderness.

Could parts of Shenandoah qualify? By almost any definition, no place in the park could be called pristine. On the other hand, using the Act's definition of "untrammeled," nearly the entire park, save Skyline Drive, had been devoid of permanent human habitation for almost three decades. The Potomac Appalachian Trail Club (PATC) quickly took up Shenandoah's cause. Noting that the Wilderness Act did "not require that a land area be clothed with virgin forest to qualify as wilderness" (a point eventually affirmed by Congress in 1975), the club argued that several large areas within park boundaries met the stated requirements. The Park Service agreed and initially identified six possible Shenandoah wilderness areas totaling nearly 62,000 acres. For skeptics, the Park Service explained that due to thirty years' growth of vegetation, "before long much of this area will be nearly identical in appearance to that observed by the first explorers."

Over the next decade, the debate over how much of Shenandoah should be designated as wilderness played out in public hearings and on the editorial pages of local newspapers. Representatives of various outdoor organizations and conservation groups (including the PATC) argued for more wilderness, while a local contingent in Madison County worried that the new designation would restrict their access to favorite sites such as Old Rag and Whiteoak Canyon. "The rich backpackers and the government," one opponent noted, "could care less [sic] about the people of Madison County."

Senator Harry F. Byrd, Jr., a frequent visitor to the park and a supporter of wilderness legislation, helped guide the political negotiations through Congress by proposing amendments that ensured local people access (via non-wilderness corridors) to their favorite

Shenandoah places. Finally, twelve long years after passage of the Wilderness Act, the 94th Congress—in its next-to-last vote before adjournment—set aside 70,019 acres of Shenandoah as wilderness, with another 560 acres to follow as soon as the park could meet certain administrative requirements. Today, 79,579 acres (42 percent of the park) are federally designated as wilderness and managed by the Park Service in compliance with the Wilderness Act. More than 175 miles of park trails, including sections of the Appalachian Trail, pass through Shenandoah wilderness. Many of the vistas on Skyline Drive take in designated wilderness areas below.

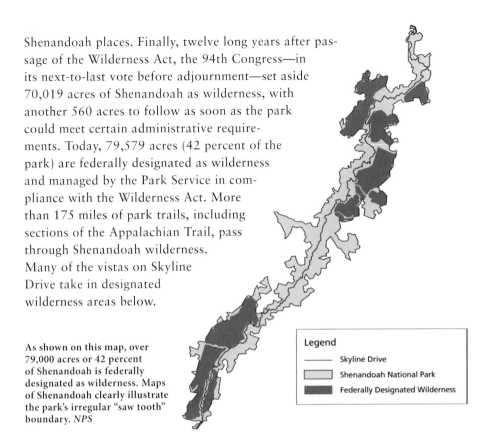

Legend

——— Skyline Drive

☐ Shenandoah National Park

■ Federally Designated Wilderness

As shown on this map, over 79,000 acres or 42 percent of Shenandoah is federally designated as wilderness. Maps of Shenandoah clearly illustrate the park's irregular "saw tooth" boundary. *NPS*

WILDERNESS TODAY AND TOMORROW

During the early decades of Shenandoah's history, many park publications characterized Shenandoah as an area that had recovered from generations of human use and abuse, where nature's regenerative powers (set free by establishment of the park) gradually returned the land to its natural state. As our understanding of park history and nature's processes grow more sophisticated, we have come to understand that in Shenandoah, as elsewhere in America, park landscapes are not so much preserved as created. Shenandoah is, as Reed Engle explains, "wilderness by design," as much a reflection of our perceptions of nature as of nature itself. Like every other human endeavor, park management is not always perfect. That does not mean, though, that Shenandoah's wilderness environment is somehow unnatural or forever tainted by human presence and influence. Indeed, in ways

Removal of dead timber with handsaws is part of Shenandoah's wilderness management program. *NPS*

both concrete and intangible, the created wilderness of Shenandoah enhances the landscape and adds value to human experience.

One immediate benefit is protection of the park's watersheds. Because the park's wilderness keeps pollutants out of Blue Ridge streams, those who live in Virginia's urban areas have suitable drinking water. Shenandoah's wilderness also provides large areas of contiguous forests for wildlife that might otherwise disappear from the region, thereby helping to maintain biodiversity. Nearly every day of the year, scientists use Shenandoah's wilderness for research in their effort to understand the planet on which we live. In addition, because wilderness has played such an important role in defining American culture, preserving wild lands nurtures our collective sense of history and provides a sense of our environmental heritage. Wilderness offers real economic benefits as well. The tourists who come to Shenandoah to experience wild country spend money in the region and studies show that rural areas bordering wilderness have higher rates of economic growth and higher property values.

The best reason for protecting Shenandoah's wilderness, however, may be less tangible. Whether one experiences it through a windshield along Skyline Drive or hiking a backcountry trail, wilderness has the power to replenish and elevate the human spirit. Senator Harry F. Byrd, Jr. understood that power. During the Senate debates on the park's wilderness bill, Byrd noted that Shenandoah "has the kind of beauty which nourishes the soul." His family, Byrd explained, had "returned to the Blue Ridge Mountains time after time to be restored in mind and body by the solitude of these ancient mountains and valleys." Each year, more than a million visitors to Shenandoah discover exactly what he meant.

Chapter IV

CHALLENGES

On Route 211, a few miles east of Luray, Virginia, the roadside scenery changes dramatically. As the highway winds up the west face of the Blue Ridge toward Skyline Drive, the area's ubiquitous strip malls, motels, and fast-food restaurants give way to tall stands of oak, hickory, and pine. A swift-flowing stream—small enough in places to step across—tumbles along beside the curvy two-lane highway. In summer, motorists turn off their car air conditioners and lower their windows to take in the scents of the surrounding forests; in winter, they turn up the heat to ward off the sudden chill. Even without the wooden signs that mark the official boundary, it is easy for drivers to tell that they have entered Shenandoah National Park. Whether one drives into the park at Front Royal, Thornton Gap, Swift Run Gap, or Rockfish Gap, the shift in ambience is invigorating, providing a sense that, at least for the duration of a park visit, the problems of urban life can be left at the foot of the mountains.

Would that it were true. For as distinct as that park boundary now seems to visitors, it is a human invention, one that often means little within the natural world. As safe and protected as it seems on a drive up from the Valley or Piedmont, Shenandoah is a park that faces new and complex challenges, many of which originate well beyond the purview of park officials.

THE "SAW TOOTH" BOUNDARY

When Congress established Yellowstone and other early western national parks, the formula was simple: Carve out large slices of unsettled (although much of it was occupied or used by Native Americans) public land and set them aside as protected areas. For Shenandoah, as for other eastern parks, it was not so easy. Nearly all the land for the park had to be acquired from private citizens. The original Shenandoah National Park Act required that a minimum boundary of 250,000 acres and a maximum of 521,000 acres be set aside. The act did not allow the National Park Service to buy any land or invoke eminent domain. Instead it left those unsavory tasks to the Commonwealth of Virginia which generally had but two options: accept land as a gift or purchase it from its rightful owner, either with or without using eminent domain, condemnation, and the forced removal of residents.

Originally, park advocates hoped to purchase some 4,000 privately held tracts for a total of half a million acres. Finally, after nine long years of political wrangling, litigation, and plans for resettlement of displaced residents, Congress and the National Park Service agreed to settle for only 180,000 acres, just over two-thirds of the initial requirement. Acquiring land for the park was rather like assembling a giant jigsaw puzzle. Virginia purchased individual tracts along the high ridges (real estate was cheaper there than in the valleys and bottomlands) and strung the property together to create the long narrow parcel that became Shenandoah.

The problem, however, was that this jigsaw puzzle had no straight pieces, nothing to frame it and give its outer border clear definition. Instead of conforming to the region's natural ecology or topography—the base of the Blue Ridge, for example—the park boundary wandered haphazardly around the lines of individual claims, creating what one park superintendent called a "saw tooth" boundary. Later land acquisitions (today the park spans roughly 200,000 acres) did little to mitigate the problem—as a glance at any modern map of Shenandoah will quickly confirm. (See park map on page 63 as evidence of a "saw tooth" boundary.)

During the first years of the park's existence, the irregular boundary created numerous headaches for Shenandoah officials. Hunters routinely trespassed in the park, illegally killing bears, deer, and other wildlife. Nearby residents grazed cattle, cut trees, and dumped garbage on parkland. By the same token, tourists and hikers often wandered onto private property, actions that incurred the wrath of local people and did little to improve relations between mountain people and the federal government. Confronted by park authorities or law enforcement, some offenders argued that trespassing was inevitable because of the complicated and unmarked boundary. It was difficult for the Park Service to disagree, especially since park staff invested hundreds of hours surveying and walking property lines, trying to determine exactly where the park ended and private holdings began.

Unlike other national parks that are surrounded by national forests or other public lands, Shenandoah remains a publicly owned island in a sea of private property. Because of the park's unique placement atop the Blue Ridge, the majority of visitors arrive from "below," driving across private tracts to reach Skyline Drive or other attractions. As a result, roadside "attractions" such as restaurants and motels (with the accompanying problems of traffic and noise) have sprung up near the most popular entry points. To gain access to certain trailheads, hikers sometimes have to cross private holdings—especially since most hikers naturally prefer to hike uphill at the beginning of their trip when they are fresh. As residential streets and subdivisions replace farmland, property owners are increasingly reluctant to tolerate park visitors near their yards and homes.

Perhaps the most serious threat from development, however, is occurring farther away, in the Virginia Piedmont and the Shenandoah Valley. In the last two decades, explosive growth and road construction in northern Virginia have made it possible for commuters to live in the western Piedmont or the Valley and drive or take public transportation into Washington, D.C., and its suburbs. Precisely because of the land's rural character and its proximity to the park, the Valley especially has become a desirable place to live. Rising land values and high property taxes often encourage those who hold farmland to sell to residential developers. If the process continues unabated, motorists on Skyline Drive might one day look down on shopping centers, subdivisions, and

Increasing development in the Shenandoah Valley and Virginia Piedmont threatens the pastoral views from Skyline Drive. *NPS*

cul-de-sacs. This problem of "viewshed protection" has no easy solution. The National Park Service has no authority over what happens on private property adjacent to the park. Expanding Shenandoah's boundaries is costly and runs the risk of alienating nearby property owners. Indeed, the relationship between the federal government and local people is still sometimes strained, in part because of the park's history and the relocation of residents in the 1930s.

As with most such problems, the solution is likely to be found in negotiation and compromise based on mutual interests. Increasingly the park works with local communities to create conservation easements and zoning regulations that allow for development, but also protect the park's natural beauty, which in turn, improves property values. In addition, groups such as the Shenandoah National Park Association and the Shenandoah National Park Trust work to enlist park supporters, raise funds, and educate the public about the importance of Shenandoah to tourism and the local economy. Such efforts are essential if Shenandoah is to retain its unique character as a place of retreat from the harried pace of modern life.

BLIGHTS

Shenandoah's magnificent woodlands have long been one of its chief resources, but like forests everywhere, those in the park are subject to disease and deterioration. Some diseases, such as common leaf spot, are native to the region and have been around long enough that trees have built up natural defenses and exist in a kind of uneasy equilibrium with the organisms that attack them. Newer diseases, especially those introduced from outside North America, can prove much more devastating. In the early twentieth century, the region's most prominent hardwood tree, the American chestnut, came under attack from a foreign contagion.

Discovered among trees at the Bronx Zoo in 1904, the parasitic fungus popularly known as chestnut blight apparently originated in Asia and was accidentally transported to America on Oriental chestnuts propagated for shade. Entering a healthy tree through a break in its bark, the alien parasite sends out threadlike tendrils that diminish the chestnut's supply of water and nutrients. In time, the fungus effectively strips a section of the tree of bark so that the limbs and leaves above die off. Spores from the fungus can be spread by wind, birds, small animals,

Chestnut blight, shown here as orange spots on this American chestnut, was first discovered on trees in the Bronx Zoo in 1904. *NPS/Mara Meisel*

insects, and even by people who walk through chestnut groves.

Before the introduction of the blight, the American chestnut had suffered from various other root fungi. The tree's original range had also been reduced through selective cutting for firewood and construction. But those problems paled in the face of the new threat. From the confines of the Bronx Zoo, the blight spread south through the eastern hardwood forests like wildfire. In Pennsylvania, foresters cleared and burned a mile-wide strip through that state's forests in a futile effort to halt the contagion. From Pennsylvania, the blight moved south across Virginia during the 1910s, traveling an estimated twenty-four miles per year.

Few trees were more useful to Appalachian people than the American chestnut. It sheltered free-roaming cattle from summer heat and storms and hogs voraciously devoured the oily nuts. Mountain folk also harvested chestnuts in autumn and shipped them to eastern cities where the nuts were roasted and sold on the street as cold-weather delicacies. In addition, chestnut lumber provided some of the best material for building construction, fence posts, furniture, and a host of other items. Tannin extracted from chestnut was crucial to the region's leather industry. As the blight swept south, those living in and around the Blue Ridge lost a crucially important forest resource.

Well before Shenandoah officially became a national park, most of the region's American chestnuts were dead or dying. The afflicted trees continued to send out new shoots from their stumps, but once they reached the sapling stage, they too became infected. The overall effect was to reduce the American chestnut from one of the Blue Ridge's most majestic trees to little more than a forest shrub. After establishment of the park, the CCC removed dead trees, especially those that might attract lightning and lead to forest fires. Road crews built some of the first guard rails for Skyline Drive from salvaged chestnut logs.

Long before Shenandoah became a national park, chestnut blight had killed thousands of trees in the area. *NPS Archives*

Foresters and conservation advocates hold out hope that a blight-resistant species of American chestnut might one day be re-introduced to Appalachian forests, including those of Shenandoah National Park. Experiments with various hybrids are ongoing and the annual sprouting of new shoots from Shenandoah's ancient chestnut stumps offer silent testimony to the tree's resilience. Perhaps future park visitors will witness the return of this magnificent denizen of the mountain forest.

Chestnut blight is not the only contagion to jeopardize Shenandoah trees. Dutch elm disease, a fungus thought to have originated in Asia and to be spread by elm bark beetles (both native and exotic), remains a problem. Of more immediate concern is dogwood anthracnose, a fungal disease first identified in New York in the 1970s. Scientists are still unsure if it is an introduced pathogen or one of native origin that has, for some reason, suddenly become a problem. The fungus seems to prey on native dogwoods that have been affected by drought or that have broken limbs and it has killed thousands of the trees within the park. Isolated dogwoods—those grown as ornamentals on private lawns for example—can be protected and treated, but it remains difficult to stem the disease's ravages in more natural settings.

PESTS

Like tree diseases, insect pests occur in virtually all forests and serve as natural agents of change. In keeping with National Park Service policy, infestations by native insects (the southern pine beetle or fall cankerworm for example) are generally allowed to run their course. Alien insects, however, pose a much greater threat and park officials generally take systematic measures to curb their impact. One such exotic insect that has been identified as a park pest since the early 1980s is the European gypsy moth.

Defoliation of oaks and other trees by gypsy moths in 2008 at Mathews Arm Campground. Fortunately, irregular outbreaks of this pest have proven relatively easy to control. *NPS*

As with chestnut blight, the importation of gypsy moths stemmed from good intentions gone awry. Originally native to Europe and parts of Asia, gypsy moth caterpillars were transported to the United States in the late 1860s as part of an effort to encourage development of a silk industry. In time, the moths slowly established themselves in the wild and eventually began to infest eastern forests. Gypsy moth caterpillars feed on leaves from some 400 varieties of American plants, but prefer white oak and associated species. Foresters estimate that 85 percent of Shenandoah's trees are at risk from the exotic pest. Park officials discovered the first gypsy moth in Shenandoah in 1969. The first serious infestation occurred in 1981. By 1986, it had caused significant loss of forest cover in the northern part of the park.

Fortunately, the gypsy moth is easier to control than some other pests. Infestations tend to be eruptive—they usually occur sporadically and for finite periods—and seem to be limited by a variety of environmental factors including weather and forest fires. Healthy trees can sometimes survive an initial defoliation by the moth's caterpillars until the infestation passes. Moreover, in years of abundant spring rainfall, gypsy moth populations appear to be impeded by the presence of a native fungus, a biological check that has helped limit Shenandoah infestations. Perhaps most important, the moths can be controlled by aerial spraying of naturally occurring bacteria that target the moth's digestive system. It is not harmful to humans, pets, or desirable insects. Though the park may never be able to rid itself of the gypsy moth, officials continually monitor its presence and seek to limit its damage, especially along Skyline Drive.

A far greater threat is another exotic pest: the hemlock woolly adelgid. Apparently native to Asia, the adelgid is a primitive insect less than one-sixteenth of an inch long. It attacks the eastern hemlock by injecting the tree with toxic saliva. The substance disrupts natural growth patterns and generally kills the tree within four to six years. First identified in the 1920s, the adelgid seemed to pose little threat until the late 1990s and early 2000s when its numbers exploded in eastern forests. Some entomologists believe the dramatic outbreak might be owing to air pollution. Long-term exposure to certain pollutants generates excessive nitrogen in eastern hemlocks, an element on which the adelgid thrives.

Hemlock woolly adelgids show up on the trees in white stringy nests. *NPS*

Unlike the gypsy moth, the hemlock adelgid has been difficult to control. In order to be effective, any pesticide must be thoroughly applied to individual trees or their roots, rendering aerial spraying essentially useless. Experiments with natural insect predators from Asia show promise, but some entomologists are leery of introducing still more exotic bugs into park forests. By 2010, 95 percent of Shenandoah's eastern hemlocks had died. The best that park officials can do is to treat and preserve individual hemlock stands in an effort to protect the gene pool until entomologists develop an effective defense against the adelgid.

As of 2010, roughly 95 percent of Shenandoah's eastern hemlocks had been killed by the hemlock woolly adelgid. *NPS*

To understand just how devastating the hemlock woolly adelgid can be, Shenandoah visitors need only venture to the popular Limberlost Trail at Milepost 43 in the Skyland area of the park. One of Shenandoah's most accessible trails, Limberlost once wound its way through an expansive stand of lofty eastern hemlocks. On hot summer days, the cool air beneath the

A hiker (insert) enjoys the Limberlost Trail before the hemlock woolly adelgid infestation. Today (background) most of the hemlocks have been killed by adelgids and removed by park personnel. *Insert: NPS Background: NPS/John F. Mitchell*

evergreen canopy was refreshing and full of birdsong. Ferns and other lush vegetation flourished on the damp shady forest floor. Due to the adelgid infestation, however, most of the trees along the trail died and were cut down for the safety of the visitors. The moist habitat on the forest floor is filling in with sun-loving plants. Stands of dead and dying hemlocks can also be observed from various overlooks on Skyline Drive. Nature, of course, will go on in some form and it remains to be seen what sort of vegetation will replace the dead hemlocks. For now, however, it is impossible not to lament the loss of these beautiful statuesque trees.

OTHER INVADERS

Insects are not the only alien organisms to take up residence in Shenandoah. In 1784, a Pennsylvania gardener acquired an exotic Chinese tree now known to botanists as *Ailanthus altissima*. No doubt the gardener knew it by its more alluring common name: the Tree of Heaven. In later years, Chinese immigrants to California also planted *Ailanthus* in the American West. From that point the story is familiar. The tree escaped from ornamental gardens and took up residence in the wild, where it soon became a problem. The first surveys of plants in Shenandoah, done in the 1930s, noted that *Ailanthus* had already become well established in the park.

Several factors make the Tree of Heaven a particularly dangerous invasive plant. First, it thrives on disturbed or open ground, meaning that it can colonize any patch of Shenandoah forest left open by a fire, windstorm, or other natural clearing agent. It grows fast and can reach a height of eighty feet. The tree's leaves produce a toxin that disrupts growth in other plants and it can quickly restrict biodiversity in any area it inhabits. As if that were not enough, the tree also emits an offensive odor, a trait that earned it the less seductive common name of "stink tree." Small wonder, then, that *Ailanthus* is now one of the Park Service's "targeted invasive species," treated with herbicides and subject to removal wherever it is found.

In 2003, park scientists conducted an extensive survey of non-native plants along Shenandoah's boundary. In addition to the Tree of Heaven (the most common invasive tree), the survey documented forty-two other species of non-native plants, including Japanese honeysuckle— the most prominent invasive shrub—and garlic mustard and Japanese stilt grass, some of the most pervasive non-native forbs. Kudzu can also be found in small patches along the park's eastern border. Although fifteen different invasive plants, including *Ailanthus*, occurred in wilderness areas, most of the invaders seem to be associated with the trappings of human civilization, frequently cropping up near areas of extensive development outside the park. At present, roughly one-fifth of all plant species found in the park are classified as non-native.

Ailanthus altissima, the Tree of Heaven, the most common invasive tree in Shenandoah. Studies of the vegetation done in the 1930s found that the non-native tree was already well established in the park. *Wikimedia. Photographer: H. Zell*

People have also had a hand in bringing exotic animals into Shenandoah. In 1890, a group known as the American Climatization Society set out to introduce to America every bird mentioned in the works of William Shakespeare. Among those birds were a hundred European starlings released in New York's Central Park. Today, the American population of European starlings is estimated at 200 million, some of which annually inhabit the area around Big Meadows. Although they can compete with woodpeckers and other cavity-nesting birds, starlings remain a relatively benign import to the park, annoying primarily in their numbers and noise.

Similarly well-meaning conservationists introduced brown and rainbow trout into Appalachian streams around the turn of the century and stocking of the two exotic fish (browns hail from Europe, rainbows from the American West) intensified during the 1930s and 1940s. To date, populations of both fish have been fairly restricted in Shenandoah, confined to the lower reaches of several streams within and just outside the park. Fisheries biologists are ever vigilant, however, for like nearly all introduced plants and animals, the non-native fish have demonstrated the ability to out-compete indigenous brook trout for food and habitat, especially in streams with warmer temperatures and poorer overall water quality.

TROUBLE ON THE WIND

From the time National Park officials first laid out Shenandoah's boundaries, clear vistas, crisp air, and streams teeming with trout have been among its top attractions. Over the last three decades, however, those valuable assets have been threatened by air pollution originating from sources both local and distant. Shenandoah is not the only national park to suffer from airborne pollutants, but its unique location atop the Blue Ridge and its proximity to urban areas have put it at greater risk than other locales.

Air pollution is a complex phenomenon, influenced not only by the actions of people, but also by the whims of nature. Generally speaking, pollutants in the air above Shenandoah take one of three forms: sulfur dioxides, nitrogen oxides, and ozone. The main sources of sulfur dioxide are coal-fired electricity-generating power plants and other industrial operations well outside the park's boundaries in Virginia, West Virginia, Ohio, Pennsylvania, and Kentucky. From largely unregulated smokestacks, the pollutants make their way into Shenandoah on prevailing easterly winds. Nitrogen oxides affecting the park come from car exhausts and other gasoline-powered machinery both in and outside the park. Ozone results from a chemical reaction between nitrogen oxides and other organic compounds in the presence of sunlight. Naturally occurring ozone in the upper atmosphere helps protect the earth from damaging ultraviolet rays, but at lower levels, ozone concentrations produced by human activity are major contributors to poor air quality.

In national parks, as in cities, all three pollutants can adversely affect human health. However, due to changing weather conditions, concentrations of the various pollutants vary, making for good and bad "air days" in Shenandoah. At present, good days still far outnumber bad (Shenandoah's high for a single year is twenty-four bad air days), but, to be on the safe side, park officials—much like urban meteorologists—occasionally find it necessary to caution visitors about high ozone levels and other forms of air pollution that can affect outdoor activities.

Researchers at Shenandoah constantly monitor air quality within the park. *NPS/ John F. Mitchell*

Atmospheric pollutants also have a dramatic effect on visibility in Shenandoah. Although other factors (including smoke, dust, and humidity) frequently restrict views from the park's overlooks and trails, air pollution is now recognized as a major contributor to the hazy skies that obscure the Valley and Piedmont, especially on hot summer days. Scientists estimate that, on average, the visual range—essentially how far the human eye can see—is about twenty-three miles. Estimates of natural visibility indicate that, without the impact of pollutants, the average visual range might be as high as 115 miles. Historical accounts suggest that it was once fairly common to glimpse the buildings of Washington, D.C., from the crest of the Blue Ridge, a view that has virtually disappeared as airborne particles have accumulated in the atmosphere. Lower-level ozone also affects plant and tree growth. Among the trees most likely to suffer from prolonged exposure to ozone are white ash, yellow poplar, and black cherry. Indeed, some predictive models show a 50-percent reduction in white ash trees in certain forests if ozone levels continue unabated.

Airborne pollutants cause even greater problems when they fall to the ground. Miles above Shenandoah, in the upper atmosphere, nitrogen oxides and sulfur dioxides mingle with moisture and sunlight to form nitric

As this composite photograph of good and poor visibility shows, views in Shenandoah can be greatly affected by atmospheric pollutants and weather conditions. *NPS*

Leaves showing damage from prolonged exposure to excessive ozone. *NPS*

and sulfuric acid. Those substances in turn mix with rain, snow, and clouds or simply drop back to earth as part of a complex process that science calls acid deposition. Most people refer to it simply as acid rain.

Acid deposition can affect tree growth, but the greatest risk at present is to the park's trout streams. All solutions, including the various creeks and runs that cascade down Shenandoah slopes, have what scientists call "acid-neutralizing capacity" or ANC. A given stream's ANC depends mostly on its natural pH, science's primary measure of acidity. A high pH means more alkaline water and a greater ability to neutralize acid; low pH means less buffering capacity. In Shenandoah, stream pH is influenced by various factors, including the topography of a given watershed and the bedrock over which the stream flows. Generally speaking, small headwater streams, the very waters most favored by eastern brook trout—which are among the most acid-tolerant of the park's native fish—tend to have lower pH and ANC. During periods of heavy precipitation or snowmelt, such streams are especially subject to rapid acidification from rainwater. That process not only threatens the trout but also other organisms, including salamanders and the insects on which the fish feed. Roughly 60 percent of Shenandoah's watersheds fall into this category.

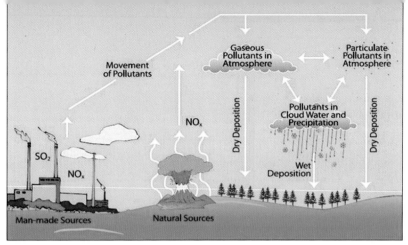

Pollutants from various sources contribute to acid deposition problems in Shenandoah. *Environmental Protection Agency*

Nature's complexity makes it difficult to gauge and even more difficult to predict the long-term effects of acidification in park streams. Acid deposition affects the soils of watersheds, limiting their ability to neutralize runoff from precipitation. Some evidence indicates that those problems may not be completely reversible, even if acid deposition can somehow be eliminated. Moreover, a trout stream is a living ecosystem, subject to myriad influences such as drought, flood, and temperature shifts, all of which can be detrimental to aquatic life. Even if low ANC itself is not responsible for fish mortality, it can weaken brook trout so that other factors take a heavier toll. At present, brook trout still live in the majority of the park's most acidified streams, but scientific models suggest that, unless air pollution and acid deposition are brought under greater control, roughly half of Shenandoah's watersheds will be in danger of losing those fish populations in the coming decades.

Fortunately, park personnel have long been diligent in monitoring the effects of air pollution and acid deposition in the park. In addition, federal legislation passed in 1977 and 1999 requires states to move toward eliminating air pollution as a source of visibility impairment in threatened parks and wilderness areas, including Shenandoah. Data collected from various locales in the park indicate slow, but tangible, progress toward this goal. Over the last three decades, amendments to the Clean Air Act and the efforts of various federal and state agencies have led to steadily declining levels of sulfur and nitrogen deposition in the park. Although ozone levels increased during the 1990s, by 2010 trends showed that concentrations of that pollutant in and around the park were also stabilizing. Even so, Shenandoah remains one of the five or six national parks most at risk from airborne pollutants.

Researchers monitor Shenandoah streams in an effort to understand the effects of acid deposition on eastern brook trout. *NPS*

THE FUTURE IS IN OUR HANDS

Without question, Shenandoah as we know it is a park at risk in the modern world. Many difficult tasks lie ahead. Curbing development on lands adjacent to park boundaries will likely require an extensive education campaign to inform property owners of the long-term benefits that accrue from preserving rural and wild land. Protection for forests from disease and invasive species will mean constant monitoring and carefully considered measures of biological and chemical control. Ultimately the solutions to air pollution and acid deposition will likely be found in government policies and individual choices geared toward cutting back on the toxins that spew from power plants and automobiles. For Shenandoah, a park dependent on the Skyline Drive and automobile tourism, those will be especially important and difficult decisions.

More than anything, though, Shenandoah needs friends and supporters—people who cherish their experiences in the park and want to see it preserved for future generations. Fortunately the park's circle of friends is large and growing. Groups such as the Shenandoah National Park Association, the Potomac Appalachian Trail Club, and the Shenandoah National Park Trust labor tirelessly to promote the park and protect its resources. A dedicated corps of park personnel—rangers, biologists, managers, and educators—know more about the park than at any time in the past. Volunteers from all walks of life routinely assist Shenandoah employees with everything from routine trail maintenance to scientific studies of forests and invasive plants.

Keeping those efforts going will require financial commitment and long-range planning. Some of the necessary funding for such endeavors will come from Congress, but increasingly national parks discover that they must augment government allocations with donations from private organizations and individuals. Whether we contribute money, time, or simply our enthusiasm for the Blue Ridge landscape, all visitors to Shenandoah can do their part to ensure a future filled with breathtaking vistas, clean air, and healthy forests that sustain native fish and wildlife. In so doing, we will be carrying on a long tradition, for Shenandoah has always been a place where people and nature combine to produce something unique, something well worth protecting.

SELECTED SOURCES

General Works on Environmental History and the Appalachians

Silver, Timothy. *A New Face on the Countryside: Indians, Colonists, and Slaves in South Atlantic Forests, 1500–1800*. New York: Cambridge University Press, 1990.
———. *Mount Mitchell and the Black Mountains: An Environmental History of the Highest Peaks in Eastern America*. Chapel Hill: UNC Press, 2003.
Steinberg, Ted. *Down to Earth: Nature's Role in American History*. New York: Oxford University Press, 2002.

General Works on National Parks and Tourism

Louder, David. *Windshield Wilderness: Cars, Roads, and Nature in Washington's National Parks*. Seattle: University of Washington Press, 2010.
Nash, Roderick. *Wilderness and the American Mind*, 4th ed. New Haven: Yale University Press, 2001.
Sutter, Paul S. *Driven Wild: How the Fight Against Automobiles Launched the Modern Wilderness Movement*. Seattle: University of Washington Press, 2004.

Shenandoah National Park History and Policy

"Acid Rain in Shenandoah National Park, Virginia." U.S. Geological Survey Fact Sheet: July 2007.
Arsenault, Matthew, Nicholas Fisichelli, et. al. "Shenandoah National Park Boundary Nonnative Plant Survey: 2003 Preliminary Results," *Newsletter of Shenandoah National Park Resource Management*, 1 (Spring 2004), 1–6.
Badger, Robert L. *Geology of Skyline Drive Shenandoah National Park, Virginia*. Shenandoah National Park Association, 2004.
Crandall, Hugh and Reed Engle. *Shenandoah: The Story Behind the Scenery*. KC Publications, 1990, 2006.
Dale, Diane M. "The Boundary Dilemma at Shenandoah National Park," *Virginia Environmental Law Journal*, 16 (Summer 1997), 607 ff.
Lambert, Darwin. "Shenandoah National Park: Administrative History, 1924–1976," copy in Shenandoah National Park Archives.
Reich, Justin. "Re-Creating the Wilderness: Shaping Narratives and Landscapes in Shenandoah National Park," *Environmental History*, 6:1 (January 2001), 9–117.
Shenandoah National Park (U.S. National Park Service), http://www.nps.gov/shen/. (See especially the work of Reed Engle at http://www.nps.gov/shen/historyculture/places.htm.)
What's Up with the Air? Shenandoah National Park. Luray, VA: Natural Resources Branch Division of Natural and Cultural Resources, Shenandoah National Park.

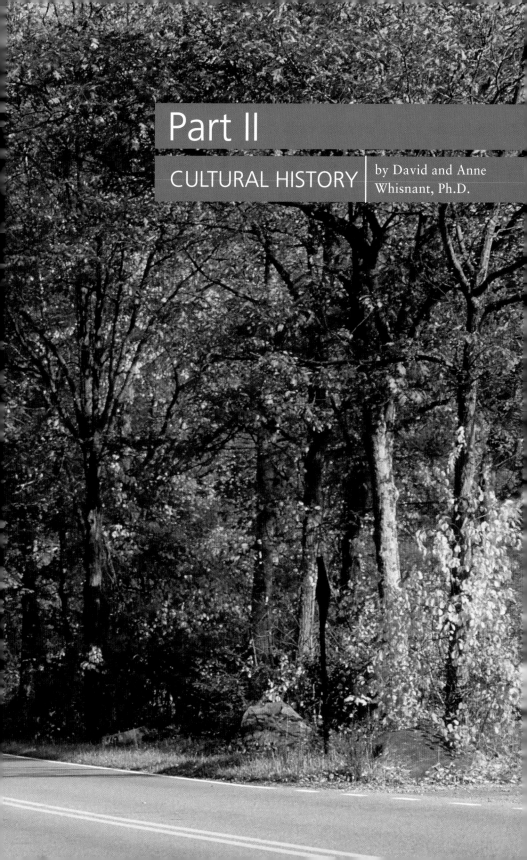

Part II

CULTURAL HISTORY

by David and Anne
Whisnant, Ph.D.

Chapter I

A NEW PARK ON OLD LAND: CREATING SHENANDOAH

On July 3, 1936, President Franklin D. Roosevelt stood on a flag-draped stage at Big Meadows and dedicated the new Shenandoah National Park. The United States Marine Band, brought from the nation's capital for the gala occasion, provided appropriately grand music.

Hundreds of local residents and dignitaries came to Big Meadows to witness the arrival of President Roosevelt's motorcade. *NPS Archives*

On July 3, 1936, FDR dedicated Shenandoah National Park to "this and to future generations." *NPS Archives*

Roosevelt celebrated the conservation of human and natural resources of which the new park was a part, and envisioned an end to "the waste of our land." He spoke hopefully of "other Shenandoahs" that would be good for the bodies and souls of yet other families. The president closed with "the ancient tale of the giant Antaeus, who, every time he touched his mother earth, arose with strength renewed a hundredfold." We seek to pass on to our children, Roosevelt said, "a richer land—a stronger nation."

It was an inspiring vision, fitting for a park that had taken a dozen years and the labor of many hands to bring into being. Its roots reached back much further than that, however. Shenandoah actually came rather late in the history of our national parks, and of ideas about how great public parks should look and function.

THE LONG ROAD TO SHENANDOAH

The first effort to establish a national park in the southern Appalachian Mountains emerged from the Appalachian National Park Association, formed in Asheville, North Carolina, in 1899. As a Virginia Congressional representative, Virginia Governor Harry F. Byrd's uncle Henry D. Flood (1865–1921) supported legislation as early as 1901 to "Establish a National Park in the East."

Another quarter-century passed before the Congress—at the urging of Park Service Director Stephen Mather and Interior Secretary Hubert Work—appointed a Southern Appalachian National Park Committee (SANPC) to search for an actual site. But a dozen more years of hard work—slowed by the economic and social disruption of the Great Depression—lay between the first Shenandoah-focused efforts in 1924 and the dedication of the park in 1936.

Soon after SANPC was formed, nearly two dozen groups besieged its members with proposals for where the new park should be. On foot and horseback, SANPC members trekked through the mountains of

George Freeman Pollock (front, left) hosted the Southern Appalachian National Park Committee (SANPC) at Skyland in 1924. *NPS Archives*

SANPC inspected, by horseback and on foot, the proposed Blue Ridge area before recommending it for inclusion in the National Park system. *NPS Archives*

Pollock and Shenandoah Valley, Inc. went to considerable expense erecting special viewing towers for the committee's visit. *NPS Archives*

Virginia, West Virginia, Georgia, North Carolina, Tennessee, and Alabama, looking for the best site. In November and December 1924, at the behest of Shenandoah Valley, Inc. (an umbrella organization formed by local chambers of commerce), some SANPC members returned to Skyland for a week-long tour of the Blue Ridge, riding over trails quickly prepared by Skyland proprietor George Freeman Pollock and viewing dramatic scenery from towers built especially for their use. A month later, SANPC reported that the Blue Ridge seemed the most appropriate site.

Those who had argued for other locations (especially the Great Smoky Mountains and Mammoth Cave) were not ready to give up, however. In February 1925, a "three parks" compromise bill upgraded the SANPC from "committee" to "commission" and gave it a bit of money to scout possible boundaries in the three contending areas. But the bill did not either establish a park or appropriate any money for one. Those hurdles were still to come.

To help shape public and official opinion in favor of the Blue Ridge, Pollock hosted the May 1925 meeting of the National Conference of State Parks at Skyland.

Meanwhile, in both the Blue Ridge and the

The "Buy an Acre" campaign was one of the first fundraising efforts by the Shenandoah National Park Association. *NPS Archives*

Smokies, the race to raise money to buy parklands began. The Shenandoah Valley Regional Chamber of Commerce and Shenandoah Valley, Inc. established the Shenandoah National Park Association (SNPA) to raise funds for the park—partly by asking the public to "Buy an Acre" for six dollars. Still unwilling to be counted out, the Mammoth Cave group also started its own fundraising effort.

Skyland was also the site of the 1925 National Conference of State Parks. Stephen Mather, director of the National Park Service (third from left, front row), was among the attendees. *NPS Archives*

The new park would be, declared SNPA President Colonel H. J. Benchoff in the *New York Times* in February 1926, "the only spot in the United States from which the visitor can look down upon the birthplace of eight presidents" as well as the "arcadian serenity" of the Shenandoah Valley. The *Richmond Times-Dispatch* ran a series on the western parks, with photos showing that the Blue Ridge was just as dramatic and beautiful. Before the end of April, SNPA had received $1.2 million in pledges.

On April 9, 1926, SANPC recommended a boundary of 521,000 acres for Shenandoah National Park, 704,000 acres for Great Smoky Mountains National Park, and 70,618 acres for Mammoth Cave. President Coolidge signed the legislation for the Shenandoah and Great Smokies parks on May 22, and for Mammoth Cave three days later.

The legislation was a milestone, but there was a catch: only when non-federal money had purchased sufficient lands would Congress authorize formation of the park (or parks). For Shenandoah, the threshold was 250,000 acres of ridgetop lands "typifying the best national park features of the region."

SHENANDOAH'S TEAM: ZERKEL, CARSON, AND BYRD

Fortunately for the park, the Virginia effort was guided by a small group of highly energetic and determined men: SNPA Executive Secretary Ferdinand Zerkel, Governor Harry F. Byrd, and Virginia Conservation Commission Chairman William E. Carson. Skyland owner George Freeman Pollock—moved as usual by both self-interest and public spiritedness—also continued to thrust himself forward. Still, "Buy an Acre" pledges were one thing, it turned out, but money in hand was another—not to mention signed deeds. The Virginia group clearly had a long row to hoe.

Ferdinand Zerkel proved to be, as park historian Reed Engle later described him, a "workhorse"—"a good and decent man with few pretensions and boundless enthusiasm" for the park, despite having to struggle constantly to support his family. Zerkel's real estate office in Luray served as the Shenandoah National Park office until 1939.

William Carson's personal financial situation was much better, and he was well connected politically. Coming to Virginia from Ireland as a boy of fifteen, he later took over his father's lime company at Riverton. He held important positions with several World War I-era federal agencies, and managed Harry Byrd's winning gubernatorial campaign in 1925. As governor, Byrd appointed him chairman of Virginia's new Commission on Conservation and Development. Unlike Zerkel, Carson was single-minded, politically ambitious, and rather authoritarian (arrogant, some found him), but he was also smart, energetic, visionary, and effective.

Harry F. Byrd had spent many days (including his honeymoon) in his family's "Byrd's Nest" cottage at Skyland. Like Carson, Byrd had risen rapidly as a young man, managed his father's newspaper (and others) and the local Southern Bell company, served as president of the Valley (Winchester to Staunton) Turnpike Company, and at twenty-five began to build an apple orchard empire that within five years made him a millionaire. An avid hiker and hunter, Byrd—who became governor in 1926—loved the Blue Ridge and was deeply committed to bringing economic development (especially tourism) to the state. The Commonwealth should be run as "a great business corporation," he declared. The proposed Shenandoah park, Byrd believed, would "attract an income to the state equal to many industries."

Byrd, Carson, and Zerkel proved to be a formidable team. "Without the political clout of Byrd and his political machine and the brilliant organizational skills of Carson," park historian Reed Engle concluded, "there would not have been a Shenandoah National Park."

Skyland's George Freeman Pollock was helpful in some ways as well. He built the new trails and towers for visiting dignitaries at his own expense, and he tirelessly promoted the project. But his entrepreneurial ambition also led him to play rather fast and loose with the truth as he joined others to work toward creating the park.

Responding to an SANPC questionnaire designed to help evaluate the deluge of proposals for park locations, Pollock and two of his Skyland associates claimed that their section of the Blue Ridge was "absolutely free from commercial development," despite decades of farming, timber cutting, tan bark gathering, charcoal making, agricultural usage, and exploratory copper mining. Hoping the Park Service would purchase Skyland and employ him to manage it, Pollock also disparaged residents of nearby Corbin Hollow in order to magnify his own efforts to "improve" their lives by hiring them at Skyland.

Fortunately, Carson and Zerkel rather than Pollock led the effort to create the park.

HOW LARGE A PARK? ESTABLISHING A BOUNDARY AND RAISING MONEY FOR LAND

Carson and Zerkel faced several difficult questions: Where should the boundary be? How much money could be gathered, and from whom? Which lands were most appropriate? And how would choosing certain lands over others affect the difficulty (and cost) of buying needed lands?

Unlike North Carolina, which was busy assembling both state and private funds for the Great Smoky Mountains National Park, Virginia declined to make state funds available, since Governor Byrd steadfastly opposed state indebtedness. In 1926, Byrd established the Virginia Commission on Conservation and Development (with Carson as chair) and focused it on the Shenandoah project. He directed Carson to move quickly to collect pledges and buy land.

Carson and others had estimated earlier that the necessary land might be bought for $2 million, but as he and six helpers surveyed and appraised some 5,000 tracts within the hoped-for 521,000-acre park, they realized that it would probably cost three times that. And only about a third of the pledged funds were in hand.

Seeing the difficulties, Carson recommended cutting the size of the park in half, eliminating both higher-priced and more heavily populated

President Hoover offered himself as "a sort of signpost" for the proposed park and held a one-time press event at Rapidan Camp. *NPS Archives*

In August of 1933, FDR visited the CCC camp in Big Meadows. He used the occasion to publicize the work-relief program. *NPS Archives*

lands as well as others not suitable for the park. By early 1927, Carson had collected about 10,000 of the 22,000 pledges he had in hand.

As late as October 1927, the actual boundary of the new (smaller) park still had not been chosen, but prospects for getting together the needed money seemed good. Carson had collected $2 million in pledges, and was trying to arrange a joint national funding campaign with Great Smoky Mountains boosters. In December, after personally inspecting the area, NPS Director Arno Cammerer recommended a new 326,000-acre boundary (the "Cammerer line"). Lobbied strongly by Governor Byrd, the Department of the Interior agreed to Cammerer's boundary.

After John D. Rockefeller gave $5 million to buy land for the Great Smokies park early in 1928, the coordinated Shenandoah-Great Smokies fund-raising campaign fell apart. At Governor Byrd's urging, however, the Virginia House of Delegates in March 1928 appropriated $1 million from state surplus funds to buy land. Two weeks later, delegates passed the Public Park Condemnation Act, easing the laws by which land for parks could be acquired. Newspaper articles promoted the park, schoolchildren contributed their pennies, and businessmen and professionals pledged substantial sums.

Despite the arrival of new funds, the Cammerer boundary did not last long. With the advent of the Depression in late 1929, Shenandoah's minimum target acreage fell still further to 160,000 acres.

At the same time, however, several promising developments increased state, regional, and national attention to the effort to create the park. The Circuit Court rejected challenges to the state's new Public Park Condemnation Act, apparently smoothing the way for land acquisition. And plans for the Appalachian Trail, under discussion since 1921, also heightened public interest in the Blue Ridge.

Probably most importantly, President Herbert Hoover—from the vantage point of his new summer fishing camp on the Rapidan River— became increasingly interested in the Shenandoah area and especially in building Skyline Drive (an idea first advanced as early as 1924 but mostly dormant since). Encouraged by Carson, the president freed federal drought relief funds to begin building the road, which in turn heightened public interest in the new park, whose "greatest single feature" the road would prove to be.

After Hoover's defeat in 1932, his interest in and advocacy for the new park passed to Franklin D. Roosevelt, who quickly proved his commitment to both Skyline Drive and Shenandoah National Park. Roosevelt established the nation's second and third Civilian Conservation Corps (CCC) camps on Skyline Drive and made a well-publicized visit to one of them in 1933.

Meanwhile, between the advent of the Depression in 1929 and Roosevelt's visit to the CCC camp, things moved slowly. Challenges to Virginia's parkland condemnation statute continued beyond the Circuit Court (eventually to the Supreme Court), and the practical and financial difficulties of acquiring the necessary lands seemed endless.

In August 1934, Virginia delivered deeds to nearly 1,100 tracts valued at $2.3 million to the federal government. But the battle for parklands was not yet over. Landowner Robert Via carried his own protest all the way to the Supreme Court, and removing some 2,300 residents still on parklands when the deeds were transferred presented unforeseen difficulties.

THE VIA CASE

In November 1934, Robert Henry ("Bob-Vi") Via filed the *Via v. Virginia* case in the U.S. District Court for the western district of Virginia. Before it was settled just over a year later, it seriously threatened the establishment of the park.

Via had large holdings in livestock, farming, timbering, and distilling operations (the latter based on the large quantities of whiskey- and brandy-making sugar hauled up Moormans River). His family had been in Virginia at least 200 years, and he was not about to give up his 154 Albemarle County acres without a fight. Via, known locally as the "King of Sugar Hollow," was a shrewd businessman. Via's suit claimed that Virginia's condemnation of his land was unconstitutional under the due process and equal protection clauses of the Fourteenth Amendment, and that the state had no power to condemn land and convey it to the federal government. An additional case filed in the Supreme Court of the District of Columbia sought to prevent Interior Secretary Ickes from accepting the parkland deeds already conveyed to him.

The District Court ruled against Via in January 1935, but he immediately appealed to the U.S. Supreme Court. Virginia argued that it was a state matter over which federal courts had no jurisdiction, but the justices agreed to hear the case in mid-November. Within a few days, they dismissed Via's appeal (*Via v. State Commission on Conservation & Development*, 296 U.S. 549; 56 S. Ct. 245), clearing the way for the park to be officially established on December 26, 1935.

Settling the *Via* case in the state's favor removed the last obstacle to obtaining clear title to the necessary land for the park. Relocating the approximately 500 families still living within the park boundary remained as a challenge, but meanwhile planning and developing the park could move ahead.

WHAT KIND OF "NATURE," WHAT KIND OF SERVICES? DEVELOPING SHENANDOAH

Since a great deal of work had already been done on Skyline Drive—by both road contractors and the CCC—developing Shenandoah National Park moved fairly quickly. But developing it nevertheless brought several related—and in some respects, conflicting—challenges: to design the park and its facilities and services (whatever it was decided they should be) for public use; to establish a presence and identity for the park separate from the already popular Skyline Drive, while melding both into a functional whole; and to rehabilitate as a "natural" scenic area land that had for many decades been farmed, logged, and developed for many other purposes.

The popularity of the new Skyline Drive reinforced planners' predictions that the scenic roadway would be the park's "greatest single feature." *NPS Archives*

Civilian Conservation Corps enrollees spent thousands of "man hours" constructing cribbing for erosion control along Skyline Drive. *NPS Archives*

The public embraced the new drive and park. By the fall of 1935, when only thirty-four miles of Skyline Drive were opened, more than a half-million people had visited the area. The matter of where any new facilities might be built and how they would be managed remained unresolved.

Plans for eating, lodging, and other facilities were under discussion. No facilities were yet available except the previously private ones at Skyland and Panorama. Would food be served at other locations, and if so, where, and at what prices?

Three years before the park opened, chief National Park Service landscape architect Thomas Vint recommended a single gasoline station, "four or five" picnic areas with food service, and overnight lodging at Skyland and Big Meadows. Whether such facilities were to be operated by the Park Service or private concessionaires was debated at length, especially by operators of existing nearby commercial facilities who feared a loss of business.

In early 1937, the Park Service signed a twenty-year concession contract with the private Virginia Sky-Line Company "to provide, establish, maintain, and operate lodges and camps for visitors, and stores, cafeterias, barber shops, bathhouses, gasoline filling stations, automobile and saddle horse transportation facilities."

Other related questions remained: What would be sold in the gift shops, and by whom? Would there be public transportation on Skyline Drive? Would there be a toll on the road, and if so, how much? (NPS tended to favor it, but local people were mostly opposed.)

Work on new facilities—and renovation of existing ones—began quickly. Cottages at Skyland were renovated, and planning began for a lodge and cabins at Big Meadows, the "Negro Area" at Lewis Mountain, and Dickey Ridge at the northern end of the park.

For the time being, at least, the planners' choices worked well. By the end of 1937 (the park's second year), visitation on Skyline Drive and in the park had exceeded one million—the first time for any national park. Such rapid progress was not to continue for very long, however. World War II began in Europe in 1939, and the Pearl Harbor attack drew the United States into it in December 1941.

An urgent challenge during the park's early years was landscaping both Skyline Drive and the park itself: seeding or laying sod on bare ground created by construction, bringing previously altered areas back to something approximating natural conditions, screening unsightly objects and undesirable views, developing nursery beds to provide vast numbers of needed plants, and controlling erosion. Landscaping also included (unfortunately in some cases) the razing of "undesirable struc- tures" in order to "abolish all traces of human habitation... and bring about... the restoration of a wilderness preserve."

Restoring that "wilderness preserve" proved extremely difficult in some respects. The disaster of chestnut blight had no remedy, and the fight against the more recent white pine blister rust was to continue for decades, as did those against insect pests and invasive exotic veg- etation such as the Asian "Tree of Heaven." Meanwhile, fires were a constant threat, as George Freeman Pollock had learned at Stony Man Camp as early as the 1890s, and as was evident during the days of the CCC, which allocated countless hours to fire control.

An "early dream" of the park's developers, observes historian Darwin Lambert, was to re-establish "the whole primeval population" of threatened or locally extinct animals (and their habitats), including beaver, bison (last seen in 1798), elk (1855), cougars (1911), tim- ber wolves (1912), and even deer and bear, which were present but scarce. Some deer were shipped in from Michigan, bears from the Alleghanies, and wild turkeys from George Washington's birthplace. Local streams were stocked with brook trout. By the mid-1950s, the wildlife situation was much improved for many species, but reports of cougar sightings were mostly unconfirmed.

Chapter II

CABINS, TRAMPING PARTIES, AND POW-WOWS: STONY MAN AND SKYLAND

By the time Shenandoah National Park was dedicated in 1936, George Freeman Pollock had been trying for more than forty years to make a go of it in the tourist industry of the Blue Ridge. George F.'s father George H. Pollock's original dream—shared by many others at the time—had been to make a fortune in copper mining in the Blue Ridge.

Although most copper mining took place in the great deposits of Missouri and the Southwest, copper deposits in Virginia were scattered all up and down both sides of the Blue Ridge, from the edge of Grayson County in the southwest to the state's northern border. Copper was being mined in Virginia by the late eighteenth century (perhaps first in Mecklenburg County on the North Carolina border), and it continued—though never on a major scale—until after World War II. By the time Virginia's last copper mine (Toncrae in Floyd County) shut down in 1947, nearly 2.5 million tons had been mined.

In the mid-nineteenth century, some speculators hoped to find mineable copper in Page, Rappahannock, and Madison counties, close to what would later become Shenandoah National Park. Virginia Cliff Copper paid a million dollars for about twenty acres of copper land eventually included within the park. Companies proliferated (Shenandoah Mining Company, Virginia Cliff Copper, and Rapid Ann [Rapidan]), and a few people made a lot of money, but most did not.

In the mid-1800s, significant amounts of money were invested in copper mining in the Stony Man area; little return was realized. *NPS Archives*

One of the companies was Stony Man Mining (1858). Stony Man Copper, Dark Hollow Copper (1858), and Miners Lode Copper (1865) also attempted operations in the Stony Man area, but by the 1880s, it was clear that, although copper ore lay underground, getting it out was uneconomical. If substantial money was to be made, investors concluded, it would more likely be made on the land itself.

FROM COPPER MINES TO RESORT LIFE

George Freeman Pollock convinced his father George H. Pollock and some of his fellow investors to develop portions of their lands as a vacation resort, and soon they were selling stock in what they called Blue Ridge Stonyman Park Preserve Lands—an enterprise heavily in debt from the outset. The partners also established Blue Ridge Park Association (BRPA) to sell lots to family, friends, and investors. It seemed a reasonable idea, given the long history of resorts in the Great Valley and adjacent mountains.

George H. Pollock died in 1893, leaving his portion of the property to his son, who advertised a "Camping Party" on Stony Man for the summer of 1894, hoping to attract investors. Fewer than twenty people (mostly family members) actually showed up for the event, but the determined Pollock, bugle in hand, continued to search for paying customers. When the balance of the BRPA lands went into foreclosure, he took out a loan to buy them.

Once George F. Pollock convinced his father to convert the mining lands into a vacation resort, George H. Pollock and his partners established the "Blue Ridge Stoneyman Park Preserve Lands" to sell mortgage bonds. *NPS Archives*

But his unencumbered assets were few, and his habit of borrowing from Peter to pay Paul landed him repeatedly in court for default. When he finally gained title to the lands more than a decade later, he was actually more in debt than ever.

In the ensuing years, Pollock continued to be sued by aggrieved groups of investors, but he pushed on with his dream of a moneymaking resort.

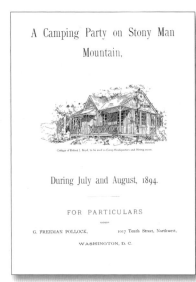

A Camping Party on Stony Man Mountain.

Cottage of Buford J. Boyd, to be used as Camp Headquarters and Dining room.

During July and August, 1894.

FOR PARTICULARS

G. FREEMAN POLLOCK,   1017 Tenth Street, Northwest,

WASHINGTON, D. C.

Above: Pollock continued to tweak his resort idea, advertising more and more extravagant seasons as the years passed. *NPS Archives*

Left: After his father's death in 1893, George F. Pollock took on the management of the resort, issuing a brochure for a "Camping Party" in 1894. *NPS Archives*

First called Stony Man Camp and finally Skyland, his resort catered to upper-middle class patrons, many from the Washington, D.C., area: doctors, federal workers, retired military officers, and businessmen.

The earliest buyers of lots at Pollock's multicultural mountainside theme park (as it seems from a later perspective) built tent platforms (sometimes with elaborate entryways), but these were soon replaced by the "rustic dwellings built of logs or frame covered with bark" specified by later deeds. Most were small and modest, though a few later ones pushed the architectural boundary.

Massanutten Lodge, built in 1911, has been restored to its original appearance and is open to visitors during the summer season. *NPS Archives*

Top left: Although early accommodations were tents, Augustus Heaton constructed an elaborate entryway. *NPS Archives*

Above: The Heatons' tents were later replaced by a small cabin, "Pines Cabin," and subsequently by the much larger "Heaton Hall." *NPS Archives*

Early buyers at the resort included Richard E. Byrd, scion of Virginia's Byrd political dynasty. For his family, artist, writer, and philatelist Augustus George Goodyear Heaton first erected a tent platform with a rather baroque rustic entranceway. He later built a cabin called The Pines, and then the much larger Heaton Hall—one of the largest ever built in the resort.

Addie Nairn Hunter (1869–1944), the divorced daughter of a Washington, D.C. real estate investor, hired renowned architect Victor Mindeleff to design her cabin at Skyland. Massanutten Lodge was completed in 1911 on two lots she

Will Grisgsby organized the Skyland dining hall, acted as Pollock's general manager, and directed the Skyland orchestra. *NPS Archives*

had bought the previous year. The virtues of her cabin and the progress of its construction were regularly reported in the local newspaper.

The charming, determined, and tireless Pollock—at once idealist and dreamer, carny and confidence man—spared neither his own effort nor his family's, friends', and investors' money to create a

Whiteoak Canyon was a favorite destination of the Skyland "tramping parties." Pollock is characteristically dressed as master of ceremonies with bugle in hand; local residents (in background) were employed as burden bearers. *NPS Archives*

resort he thought would appeal to such a clientele. It was to be a quiet mountainside retreat isolated from the bustle of urban life, where guests dressed informally, ate wholesome food, and enjoyed elaborate entertainments.

Knowing which side his bread was buttered on, the always debt-burdened Pollock forbade guests to cook in their own quarters. They had to take their meals in the dining hall, which over the years grew from fifty to 200 and finally to 300 seats. The menu ranged from eggs, bacon, and biscuits to "young lamb, fed on mountain blue grass" and (with Pollock's characteristic flair) "Chilled Black Seed Aqua Pura Massanuttona-Melona" (a.k.a., watermelon). Will Grigsby, a black cornet player from Luray, ran the dining room and directed the orchestra.

The social atmosphere was homey and constantly varied: from bonfires, music, and dancing, to healthful outdoor exercise: swimming at the resort's Kaegey Spring pool (to musical accompaniment from the small orchestra platform), ping pong and tennis, picnics and barbecues, horseback rides, and hiking ("tramping" was the preferred term) and camping trips. Resort guests also attended elaborate and exotic entertainments: carnivals, flower balls, masquerade balls, and faux Indian pow-wows.

Virginia's Mineral Springs Resorts

When George Freeman Pollock opened his Stony Man Camp (later Skyland) high in the Blue Ridge in 1894, he had reason to believe it might attract a reliable stream of guests with time on their hands and money to spend. Forty-five miles to the south at Blackrock Gap, the Blackrock Springs resort had been a going concern since the 1830s, attracting vacationers to mountain air and views, good food and lodging, a bowling alley, and outdoor entertainments.

Indeed, for more than a hundred years, summer resorts had flourished in Virginia, mostly in the Valley, but elsewhere as well. Most were associated with springs whose warm, mineral-rich waters (bathed in or taken internally) were reputed—depending upon the particular minerals present—to relieve or heal a whole alphabet of ailments: bronchitis, consumption, dropsy, nervousness, physical exhaustion, rheumatism, skin inflammation, even typhoid. Those unable to afford to travel to the resorts could buy bottled water from Rockbridge Alum, Buffalo Lithia, or White Sulphur Springs.

During their heyday (1830–1890), there were nearly one hundred such resorts in Virginia. Some (like Blue Ridge Springs, founded in 1866) were spurred by the completion of the Virginia and Tennessee Railroad from Lynchburg to Roanoke and then down the Valley to Abingdon and Bristol in 1856.

Blackrock Springs guests pose in front of the bowling alley. *NPS Archives*

Blackrock Springs Hotel accommodated three dozen guests and there were an additional thirty private cottages.

Three generations of the Byrd family frequented Skyland Resort beginning in 1905, when they purchased the cabin they called "Byrd's Nest." The family included famed explorer Richard Evelyn Byrd and patriarchs of the Virginia political dynasty Harry Flood Byrd, Sr. and Jr. *NPS Archives*

A "MARRIAGE OF OPPOSITES," AND THE LATER YEARS OF SKYLAND

By the end of the year after she arrived at Skyland, Addie Nairn had married George Freeman Pollock. It was, historian Reed Engle observed, "a marriage of opposites": a poorly educated, debt-ridden, immodest, gregarious ladies' man and a wealthy, educated, cultured, but introverted and reserved woman. They shared a love for the Blue Ridge Mountains, but almost none of their other passions intersected. Pollock no doubt saw in the marriage a potential route out of his perennial indebtedness, however, and his wife appears to have helped him pay off some liens on the property.

The marriage lasted until Addie's death in 1944, but by 1920 or so Pollock had been moved out of Massanutten Lodge. Addie attended his galas, but ate alone and preferred evenings in the lodge with a few friends. Her bequests to Pollock in a succession of wills grew ever smaller; the final one left him nothing.

Fortunately his wife was not Pollock's only source of funds. Over the years, several other major investors played key roles in sustaining and

The pre-park Panorama Tea Room was the centerpiece of the Thornton Gap entrance at Route 211 until it was razed in 1958. *NPS Archives*

developing Skyland. Western rancher and cattleman Robinson Bosler loaned Pollock money, bought lots, and built eleven cabins (including Whispering Pines). Georgia physician George Woodruff Johnston also loaned money, bought lots, built several cabins, and served as camp physician for a time. And artist Augustus Heaton built a dance pavilion and stage, helped finance a telephone line to Luray, and built Heaton Hall. One of Johnston's cabins, built before 1905, was later sold to Richard Byrd, who renamed it "Byrd's Nest." His eldest son Harry F. Byrd later bought it and spent his honeymoon there in 1913.

Pollock's latter years at Skyland were frustrating and disappointing. In mid-1924, competing Panorama Resort had opened on a 350-acre tract about ten miles away on U.S. Highway 211 that included Marys Rock. By 1928, Panorama consisted of two- to six-bedroom furnished, bungalow-style cottages; a tea room; a fourteen-room summer hotel; a 200-seat dining room; a tennis court; and a miniature golf course. The resort attracted visitors from as far away as New York.

Despite the competition and his never-ending debt, Pollock thought there was another way to save his resort. When in 1925 the Southern Appalachian National Park Committee recommended establishing a park in the Blue Ridge, he saw its coming as a possible way both to solve his financial problems (his indebtedness would total $100,000 by

Civilian Conservation Corps workers re-shingled cabins at Skyland in anticipation of the visitors who would come to the new Shenandoah National Park. *NPS Archives*

1929) and at long last to own (or at least to operate, perhaps as a Park Service concessionaire) a stable and solvent resort in the Blue Ridge.

The owners of Panorama had similar hopes, but ran afoul of NPS Director Arno B. Cammerer when in 1934 they challenged the Park Service's appraisal of their property, now inside the park boundary. A compromise allowed manager J. Allen Williams to continue operating the hotel until park concessionaire Virginia Sky-Line Company took it over in early 1937. The Park Service razed it in 1958; a cloverleaf interchange on U.S. Highway 211 now occupies the site.

Pollock was similarly buoyed by the advent of the Skyline Drive (1931–1939), which he anticipated would bring more paying guests to Skyland. By 1932, however, it was clear that his indebtedness and Park Service plans for Shenandoah would not permit him to retain ownership.

Pollock's friendly relationship with NPS Director Arno Cammerer bolstered his hope that he would be allowed to manage Skyland as a concessionaire. For several years he continued to negotiate with the Park Service, but his lack of business sense and inability (or unwillingness) to meet Park Service standards undermined his efforts. In 1937, Virginia Sky-Line Company won the concession contract.

Beginning in 1933, the Civilian Conservation Corps began work on the Skyline Drive right-of-way adjacent to Skyland. The park's early (1936) Master Plan envisioned rehabilitating and repurposing some Skyland buildings and upgrading its water and sewage system. A few buildings were torn down and bark siding on others was replaced. Some rather grandiose plans to expand the resort never materialized.

Fortunately, later plans emerging from the Park's Service's fiftieth anniversary Mission 66 endeavor also were never carried out. They called for demolishing all Pollock-era buildings in Skyland. Together with eleven other buildings that embody the fascinating but financially troubled history of Skyland, Massanutten Lodge remains, and has been restored to the 1916 time period by the Park Service. Massanutten Lodge is open to visitors through ranger-led tours and features the historically refurnished living room as it was when Addie vacationed there and an exhibit, "Women of Skyland," which tells the stories of some of the progressive and independent women who frequented Skyland Resort.

Chapter III

FINDING REFRESHMENT OF MIND: PRESIDENT HOOVER'S RAPIDAN CAMP FISHING RETREAT

Certainly one of the most historically compelling excursions available to Shenandoah National Park visitors is the one to President Herbert Hoover's Rapidan Camp.

Established in 1929, the camp served Hoover throughout his presidency as a personal summer retreat, fishing camp, and getaway for meetings with friends, Cabinet members, foreign dignitaries, and public figures. Under the trees on the banks of the Rapidan, he visited with Winston Churchill, inventor Thomas Edison, flying ace Charles Lindbergh, and pioneer auto manufacturer Henry Ford.

Rapidan Camp consisted of thirteen rustic buildings, including two mess halls, the presidential quarters ("the Brown House"), guest cabins for visitors, staff quarters, a "Town Hall" for meetings, and several service buildings.

President Hoover's rustic cabin at Rapidan, "the Brown House," was in stark contrast to his weekday home in Washington, the White House. *NPS Archives*

Marines stationed near the president's camp provided security when Hoover was at Rapidan. *NPS Archives*

A mile away there was another camp for U.S. Marine Corps personnel who built and maintained Rapidan Camp and provided security and support services. Visiting Cabinet officers stayed at a third camp two miles downstream.

Creel Cabin, once the favorite of Hoover's physician, Dr. Joel Boone, is one of the three remaining buildings at Rapidan. It has been renovated to house volunteers. *NPS Archives*

The Marine camp on the Rapidan was torn down in 1944, and remaining buildings of the Cabinet camp passed into private ownership in 1953. But several buildings and portions of the landscaped grounds of Rapidan Camp have been restored to their condition in 1930–1931. The Creel Cabin is currently used as quarters for seasonal volunteer site supervisors.

From late spring into the fall, ranger-guided tours of Rapidan Camp are available by reservation, departing from the Harry F. Byrd Sr. Visitor Center.

A GETAWAY FOR THE PRESIDENT, BUT WHERE?

Virtually since the beginning, U.S. presidents sought retreats beyond the summer heat and humidity of Washington, D.C. Several pre-Civil War presidents preferred Pennsylvania's Bedford Springs Hotel. Abraham Lincoln and Chester Arthur stayed closer by in the Soldier's Home, only three miles from (but 300 feet higher than) the White House, and Woodrow Wilson liked the New Jersey coast.

Before President Hoover came to office, President Coolidge had recommended that the government establish an official "summer White

House" not too far from Washington, where chief executives could spend weekends in a relaxed and informal atmosphere.

Hoover was intrigued by Coolidge's idea, since it promised to allow him to pursue his lifelong interest in the outdoors, and especially in fishing ("the eternal fountain of youth," he called it). He instructed one of his secretaries, longtime friend and fellow outdoorsman Lawrence Richey, to look for a site. As word of Richey's discreet inquiries leaked out, both Congress and local boosters rushed to suggest sites—including the federal Weather Mountain property near Berryville (for which Congress quickly approved improvement funds) and George Freeman Pollock's Skyland Resort.

Hearing through the grapevine (possibly from the postmaster at nearby Criglersville) that plans to find a site were afoot, Virginia State Commission on Conservation and Development chairman William Carson, then involved in raising funds and buying land for Shenandoah National Park, began corresponding directly with Hoover about a Madison County site. Excitedly speculative articles soon appeared in the county seat newspaper, the *Eagle*.

Hardly waiting for Hoover's response, Carson quickly informed him that he had already secured fishing rights from the Rapidan Fishing Club at a site on the Upper Rapidan River. Carson then called together a group of county leaders, told them about the fishing rights, and urged them to provide a necessary road and telephone lines. With little delay, the county and state came through with the former and the Chesapeake and Potomac Telephone Company with the latter.

In mid-March 1929, an inspection party (including Richey and the secretary of the interior) rode horseback from the county seat over Chapman Mountain and down to the river. As the president's personal representative, Richey approved the site, and a March 22 *Eagle* headline proclaimed "Upper Rapidan Chosen as Fishing Lodge for President Hoover."

It remained only to show the Upper Rapidan to Hoover and his wife. Since Hoover had been inaugurated on March 4, preparations (including Secret Service protection) had to be elaborate. The presidential party proceeded from Criglersville, first in Model A Fords and then by horseback. Hoover's personal physician reported later that upon arriving, the president dismounted, walked up and down the river, pointed to a plot of level land where Mill Prong and Laurel Prong creeks joined together to form the Rapidan, and said, "This is where I am going to build a cabin. This is just what I want." On April 12, the *Eagle* splashed a banner headline: HOOVER VISITS AND ACCEPTS!

DESIGNING AND DEVELOPING THE CAMP

For the president to proclaim "This is just what I want" was simple, but much of the work required to put the retreat on the ground actually fell to his superbly competent wife, Lou Henry Hoover, and to hundreds of Marines.

And a lot of ground it was. On July 20, William Carson bought 286 acres from the Wayland family (land they had held since 1828); eleven days later, he sold 164 acres of it to the Hoovers for about $25,000. The Hoovers insisted upon developing the camp out of their own money rather than accept a discreetly unpublicized offer from the state to build a $100,000 lodge for them.

Not surprisingly, Rapidan Camp turned out to resemble a Girl Scout camp, since the architect Mrs. Hoover engaged (James Y. Rippin) had served on the board of the Girl Scouts of America (GSA) with her, and had designed a GSA camp building in New York.

Mrs. Hoover asked for buildings with "good board flooring and a roof" and curtained sides, "not unlike some of the Girl Scout mess halls." There were to be two or three "sturdy shacks entirely of wood" for storage, a mess hall (with a fieldstone fireplace) to seat twenty or so people, staff work rooms, suites of guest rooms, rooms for cooks and servants, and accommodations for the Secret Service. The Hoovers' personal quarters were to include sleeping and dressing rooms, and work spaces for each of them.

Originally the Brown House had just one bedroom, but as shown by the window over Mrs. Hoover's bed, a second bedroom/office was added for the president. *NPS Archives*

The Brown House, the Hoovers' cabin, was nestled among towering hemlocks at the headwaters of the Rapidan River. *NPS Archives*

Top left: "Five Tents" was constructed for the Hoovers' first visit to their camp. Once the Brown House was completed, it became guest and staff quarters. Although it too was later wood-sided, it retained its original name. *NPS Archives*

Above: Mrs. Hoover's first instructions to the architect were for quarters to be made of wooden platforms with canvas tents. Later, wooden siding replaced the canvas. *NPS Archives*

Development of the grounds followed Mrs. Hoover's specifications closely. Even the President's Cabin had uninsulated German siding walls and no interior ceilings, and the tin-walled shower stalls had concrete floors. Hoover's first overnight was a stay in the largest (thirty-by-one-hundred-foot) building—"Five Tents"—which had a wooden floor and three-foot-high walls with five canvas tents above. All the "tents" soon became wooden cabins, succumbing to pressure from the Secret Service. "Five Tents" kept its name.

The buildings were actually constructed by Marines, who also brought in heavy road-building machinery to move boulders and build the roads—sometimes on steep slopes—from Criglersville up Quaker Run, over Chapman Mountain Ridge, and then upriver to Rapidan Camp. Timber bridges (one of them one hundred feet long) spanned the creeks. By August 2, White House cars were able to drive all the way into the camp.

After construction ended, the grounds were reshaped and landscaped according to the "constant[ly] botanizing" Lou Henry Hoover's extensive notes on "Flowers and Shrubs for the President's Camp." Some seventy-five miles of trails were carved out to peaks, waterfalls, and other scenic places. With a newly built large outdoor fireplace, a fountain, and a horseshoe pit, and the Filipino mess crew relocated from the recently decommissioned presidential yacht, all was ready for the president. It had been in every sense a cost-sharing project: state and federal governments provided personnel, equipment, and services, but the Hoovers put some $114,000 of their personal funds into it as well.

THE HOOVERS AT RAPIDAN

The Hoovers intended to use Rapidan Camp for rest and relaxation for themselves and their children, but the camp's purpose evolved as Hoover's presidency progressed. Perhaps two events in the camp's early days foreshadowed what the camp would become: a fully functional working retreat under the constant scrutiny of the public. "Hoover Day" hosted in mid-August by Hoover's Madison County neighbors

The sitting room of the Brown House was heated by an enormous fieldstone fireplace. Staff was from the decommissioned presidential yacht. *NPS Archives*

Hoover was an avid fisherman and was drawn to the Rapidan because of its reputation as an excellent trout stream. *NPS Archives*

suggested just how interested the general public was in the first family's weekend pursuits. And a successful private diplomatic encounter in early October revealed to Hoover the advantages of conducting business away from the politically charged atmosphere of Washington, D.C.

Barely two weeks after the first White House motorcade drove into Rapidan Camp, Madison County staged a "Hoover Day in Madison" to thank the president for focusing public attention on the county by selecting it, the local newspaper said, "as his summer playground." After Hoover announced that he would actually attend the event, the Madison *Eagle* predicted grandly that it would be "the biggest day in the United States of America or any of its possessions!"

Event planners engaged two bands to play and reserved the county fairgrounds and adjacent acreage to handle expected crowds. Families

"The Prime Minister's Cabin" was named in honor of the historic visit of British Prime Minister Ramsey MacDonald. *NPS Archives*

were urged to bring baskets of food, and cattle and pigs were lined up for slaughter. Five thousand tin cups were ordered to serve fifty wash pots full of squirrel stew. Several thousand cars came, and Governor Byrd arrived somewhat melodramatically in an army blimp.

"I have thought it appropriate to accept the hospitality of your citizens and your mountains for one or two days each week," Hoover told a crowd larger than the entire county's population.

> You have demonstrated yourselves good hosts and good neighbors... by lending me a part of your park, by improving a road, by securing the fishing rights on a beautiful mountain stream and even providing me with fishing tackle. I, on my side, am glad to lend my services as a good neighbor to you by acting as a sort of signpost to the country of the fine reality of your proposed new national park.

Through fishing, Hoover continued,

> Presidents... may escape to their own thoughts and may live in their own imaginings and find relief from the pneumatic hammer of constant personal contacts, and refreshment of mind in the babble of rippling brooks.

For local people, the outcome could hardly have been better. They had Hoover's "summer playground" and the press coverage that went with it, they had his public commitment to the "fine reality" of the coming national park, and the Marines had built some new hard-surface roads to replace a few of the muddy ones they were used to.

The October event was British Prime Minister Ramsay MacDonald's visit to talk with Hoover about limiting the size of navies to slow the ruinously expensive arms race between the two countries.

Arriving at the White House dressed in cutaway and striped pants, as protocol required, MacDonald was surprised to learn that he and his daughter Ishbel would be driving to Hoover's fishing camp in the mountains, where the president had prepared two cabins for his guests. Fortunately, both visitors were able to augment their clothing from the Hoovers' own closets.

The Madison *Eagle* reported (whether factually or not, no one knows) that the two men did much of their talking at Rapidan while sitting on a log overlooking the trout pond. Whatever the details, Rapidan Camp was for a short time, as historian Reed Engle observed, "the news center of the world," and the encounter led to the Naval Limitation Treaty the president signed in July 1930.

The camp was never again the scene of so publicized a diplomatic meeting, though it was used many times for official conversations and meetings amidst the "babble of rippling brooks" Hoover referred to in his Hoover Day speech. In May 1931, he called federal department heads to Rapidan to work on budget cuts. A later conference led to the formation of the Reconstruction Finance Corporation in 1932.

The *New York Times* and other newspapers carried literally hundreds of articles on the Hoovers' visits to Rapidan, where fishing, hiking, horseshoe pitching, good food, and peaceful evenings before the indoor and outdoor fireplaces relieved the stress of meetings and serious talk.

As it turned out, however, the President's Hoover Day promise to be a good neighbor to local people produced few tangible results except his continued official support for the new national park. Leaving the active neighboring to his wife, Hoover himself rarely ventured outside the camp. Fortunately, his wife took the neighboring role seriously.

Financed by the Hoovers and supervised by the local school district, the Hoover School building was constructed by local laborers. *NPS Archives*

LOU HENRY HOOVER AND HER RAPIDAN NEIGHBORS

In January 1929, before Rapidan Camp had become a reality, Lou Henry Hoover wrote to a friend about a reconnaissance trip she had made to the area. It was "gently sloping land," she reported, except where occasional cornfields or orchards had been cleared by "the primitive mountain folk."

"Primitive" was only one of many condescending terms used to refer to mountain people at the time. How Mrs. Hoover formed her impression of mountain people is not certain, but she and perhaps the president's personal physician, retired Admiral Joel T. Boone, may have read some of the then popular (though misleading) accounts of Appalachian people's lives: John Fox's *Little Shepherd of Kingdom Come* (1913), a romantic story of Kentucky mountain people, and perhaps early portions of research (also misleading) later published by Mandel Sherman and Thomas Henry as *The Hollow Folk* (1933).

Fortunately, in the months and years that followed, Mrs. Hoover demonstrated an uncommon ability to empathize with local people. On long horseback and auto excursions, she gained some understanding of their lives and helped them in a variety of ways, frequently acting (though never openly) on behalf of her husband as well.

After her visit to the Clore furniture plant in Madison (in business since 1832) was reported in the local newspaper, the company had to build an addition to fill increased orders. Later, when the plant was damaged by fire, she loaned the Clores money to help them rebuild.

The most public example of the Hoovers' concern for their mountain neighbors was the school they established for local children. Numerous colorful stories of questionable accuracy surround the origin of the project, but the essential facts about the Hoovers and their school have been sketched by park historians Darwin Lambert and Reed Engle.

THE PATRIARCH OF THE DISTRICT: MARTIN JACKSON BURRAKER,
72 Years Old, Grandfather of Rae, Who Walked Two Miles Over the Mountains With Mrs. Burraker to See Their Grandson Raise the Flag at the Opening of the School.
(Times Wide World Photos, Washington Bureau.)

The opening of the school garnered extensive media attention, much of which was focused on the mountain residents. *NPS Archives*

Miss Vest accompanied her students to the Madison County Fair. Other outings included field trips to Washington, D.C. *Jameson Photo, NPS Archives*

The school emerged first from the Hoovers' broader concern for people caught in unfortunate circumstances, and their habit of providing, for example, financial and other aid to the Girl Scouts and to young women who were trying to go to college.

Fortunately, the Hoovers became sufficiently aware of the local people and their actual circumstances to form their own independent sense of what might be helpful to them. Planning for the school had begun at least by early September 1929. The Hoovers promised to underwrite all costs, but the state Department of Education and the Madison County Board of Education helped with planning and design.

By mid-October, construction was under way, and with the help of donated materials and labor, the model building was completed in mid-February 1930. It had a classroom and living quarters on the first floor and two dormer rooms upstairs. Two large stone fireplaces provided heat, and a mountain spring supplied running water.

Several dozen newsmen turned out for the opening of the school on February 24, eager to photograph the children and interview their teacher, twenty-five-year-old Berea College graduate Christine Vest. Following popular stereotypes, press reports stressed the "backwoods" character of mountain life, "where poverty and ignorance go hand in hand." Extensive press coverage continued through the summer, featuring similarly stereotypical characterizations of students and their families. Fortunately, that coverage also moved individuals and businesses to send school materials and equipment.

Vest taught an average of about twenty students, who arrived eagerly as soon as the doors opened. She grouped them by ability rather than into the usual grades. The building also came to serve as a gathering place for community people, a night school for parents, and a place to hold Sunday religious services. Some girls stayed at night and enjoyed warm baths. Especially after the drought of 1930 began, Mrs. Hoover gave Vest money for clothes and shoes for the children, and the president ordered many barrels of flour.

After the park was established and the residents relocated, the building was later moved to Big Meadows and converted for use as a ranger station.

Herbert Hoover left office in March 1933, in the midst of unprecedented economic and social turmoil. The Great Depression began with the stock market crash of October 1929. Banks closed, businesses laid off masses of workers, and bread lines formed. At the end of July 1932, 17,000 World War I veterans and nearly as many supporters staged the Bonus Army March on Washington, demanding that the wartime bonuses promised by Congress be paid. Hoover authorized military troops to force them out of the capital at bayonet point, gassing them and burning their temporary shacks in sight of the capitol.

Against such a backdrop, Rapidan Camp was a symbolically appropriate positive legacy from a president who, whatever his failure to deal with the Depression, had added substantially to the nation's natural treasures—saving Niagara Falls through a treaty with Canada (1930), controlling oil leases and curbing overgrazing on public lands, adding more than two million acres to the national forests, and increasing the National Park system by 40 percent.

Perceived by the public as not doing enough to deal with the Depression, however, Hoover was defeated in 1932. Rapidan Camp was within the area of condemnation for parkland. Hoover did not accept payment for the property but hoped that the camp would be used by future presidents. It became part of the park in 1935.

For the most part, however, future presidents did not share Hoover's enthusiasm for the "babble of rippling brooks" on the Upper Rapidan. Franklin Roosevelt visited it in once 1933, but preferred a Maryland camp which was more wheelchair accessible. He named the camp Shangri-La (later renamed Camp David).

Meanwhile, plans to upgrade the camp for other possible uses did not come to fruition. In 1946, the park superintendent reported that it had not been used since 1941. The Marine camp was demolished in 1944, and the Boy Scouts leased Rapidan Camp from 1948 into the late 1950s. A group of private individuals bought the Cabinet camp in 1953. In 1959, the National Park Service tore down all but three Rapidan Camp buildings, whose interiors they refurbished in the early 1960s.

Presidents Truman, Eisenhower, and Johnson never visited Rapidan. A helipad at Big Meadows was prepared for President Nixon, but he never came, though some of his staff used the camp frequently. President Jimmy Carter (1977–1981) used it early in his term, and Vice President Mondale came often.

The three remaining buildings from the main camp (the Brown House, the Prime Minister's Cabin which now houses an exhibit, and the Creel Cabin), together with various landscape features, were registered as a National Historic Landmark in 1988 (under the name Camp Hoover, used by the Boy Scouts).

Rapidan Camp continued to be used as a vacation spot for government officials until 1992, when building and infrastructure deterioration made further such use impossible. Beginning in 2004, the Park Service restored Rapidan Camp to its 1930–1931 appearance. The historic site is currently open to the public and ranger-led tours are available by reservation.

Chapter IV

Many roads lead to Shenandoah National Park, but only one—spectacular 105-mile-long Skyline Drive—leads through its entire length from Front Royal on the northern end to Rockfish Gap on the southern end. There it connects with the Blue Ridge Parkway, which continues another 469 miles to Great Smoky Mountains National Park.

Talked about for years as a possibility before construction began, the ridgetop scenic road that came to be called Skyline Drive was built between 1931 and 1939—straddling the creation of Shenandoah National Park, authorized in 1926 and dedicated a decade later.

Major construction work on Skyline Drive was carried out by private contractors, but much of the detail work (shaping of slopes, landscaping, building of guard walls and rails, and preparing parking areas, campgrounds, and overlooks) was done by the New Deal's Civilian Conservation Corps (CCC), which set up its first camp in the Blue Ridge in May 1933.

A beautifully illustrated postcard showed the serpentine curves of Skyline Drive. *NPS Archives. Publisher: Marken & Bielfeld, Inc. Frederick, MD*

A ranger at the north entrance to Shenandoah National Park welcomes the first paying visitors to drive the Skyline Drive. *NPS Archives*

When the first still unpaved few miles of Skyline Drive were opened temporarily in October 1932, nearly 8,000 cars drove the road in thirty-eight days. By 1939, officials feared that travelers were "loving it to death." In that year alone, more than 270,000 vehicles traveled the road.

Elevations on Skyline Drive range from less than 1,000 feet at Front Royal to 3,500 feet at Big Meadows; the southern entrance station at Rockfish Gap lies at 1,900 feet. Hawksbill Mountain, the highest peak in the park, rises to 4,051 feet. Along the route, dozens of scenic overlooks offer splendid views eastward toward the Piedmont and westward toward the historic Shenandoah Valley.

Visitor facilities (hiking and camping, food, rest stops, picnic grounds, and lodging) are available and well marked.

IMAGINING AND BUILDING THE ROAD

Though it had recognizable antecedents in the great western park roads of the 1920s, the idea for Skyline Drive may have been first mentioned in 1924 by William C. Gregg, a member of the Southern Appalachian National Park Committee, established by Congress to look for a suitable site for the first eastern national park. On a visit to Skyland with the committee, Gregg suggested that a scenic road at or near the top of the mountain be built. In its final report, the committee recommended just such a road, which it said could be "the greatest single feature" of the contemplated park.

The spectacular fall foliage colors bring
thousands of visitors each year. *NPS Archives*

Skyline Drive did not begin as a unified aesthetic and engineering
design. Especially during the many months required for it to move
beyond a tentative and fragmentary idea, the road took shape—both
as design and as reality—through a series of not always tightly linked
steps, tapping funds along the way as opportunities opened.

Seven years passed after Gregg's suggestion before the first shovelful of
dirt was turned, and that happened not because there was a ground-
swell of public and official support for a scenic ridgetop roadway
(though such support certainly existed), but because in late 1929 the
state of Virginia began to experience an extraordinary drought.

The drought increased the need for non-farm work, so that even temporary construction jobs working on the new road seemed likely to
provide relief to farmers whose crops had been ruined. Those still able
to farm hoped the road might help them get their produce to Piedmont
or Valley markets.

Key figures in the push to begin construction were William E. Carson,
chair of the Virginia Commission on Conservation and Development,
and Ferdinand Zerkel, executive secretary of the Shenandoah National
Park Association. Both had long been occupied with planning and
acquiring land for the new park.

President Hoover, who had become acutely aware of drought conditions during his visits to Rapidan Camp, called a conference of
governors of the thirteen affected states to discuss relief measures.
Characteristically, he urged that most relief be undertaken by private
volunteer agencies such as the Red Cross, but he did propose that
Congress provide $100 million to $150 million in emergency funds for
construction projects.

Seizing the opportunity, Carson and Zerkel moved to carve out some of the emergency construction funds for Skyline Drive. Taking an indirect approach, they initially urged that a road be built between Hoover's Rapidan fishing camp and the Skyland Resort to increase presidential security and ease travel for the presidential press corps headquartered at Skyland.

During the ensuing weeks, a flurry of communications passed among interested parties: NPS Director Horace Albright, William Carson, Hoover's personal secretary Lawrence Richey, Ferdinand Zerkel, Virginia Senator Carter Glass, and Hoover himself.

Marys Rock Tunnel at mile 32.2 was bored through 670 feet of solid granite, an engineering feat in its time. *NPS Archives*

Farmers whose crops were ruined and who could neither sell nor borrow against land that was tied up in plans for the new park would welcome employment building the road, Carson and Zerkel expected, though whether they would actually get such employment soon enough to help was far from certain.

Farmers who owned land along the route seemed pleased that the road was coming, but many did not understand that road and park were a package deal, or that once the park came they would not be able to continue either to farm or to live on their land.

Carson proposed a road from the Panorama Resort on the Lee Highway (U.S. Highway 211) to the Rapidan Valley road (built by state money for the president's convenience in getting to Rapidan Camp). By the end of January 1931, the requested funds had been released. This initial segment of the road, lying approximately in the middle of the proposed park, became the first two sections of Skyline Drive (IA and IB), from Thornton Gap to Swift Run Gap.

By April 1931, the center line of the new roadway had been surveyed and some tracts for the one-hundred-foot right-of-way were being bought, but the Park Service warned that unless surveying, appraising, and clearing of titles were complete by July 1, the project could not go forward.

Skyline Drive opened temporarily to rave reviews on October 23, 1932. *NPS Archives*

Eventually some 12,500 acres were acquired for these two initial segments. Parcels ranged from three to more than 1,200 acres, at an average cost of about seventeen dollars per acre. Total cost was under $700,000—$100,000 less than estimates.

On June 25, just before the deadline, construction began on Section IA, from Panorama to Big Meadows. The next day, the machinery rumbled again as Section IB (Big Meadows to Swift Run Gap) got under way.

There was as yet no unified plan for a long ridgetop road, however. Ideas differed amongst officials and agencies, and deliberations were complicated still further by resistance from Appalachian Trail (AT) partisans, who feared that a ridgetop road would degrade or even over-run sections of their new trail.

Zerkel, clearly irritated, found the AT objections presumptuous. The road would be the all-important artery, he declared; the trails would be the veins. AT resistance abated for a while, but it did not go away.

Compared to the altitudes of some roads built in the western parks in the 1920s (above 6,600 feet at Logan Pass on the Going to the Sun Road in Glacier National Park) those of the projected Skyline Drive were modest. Nevertheless, contractors had to contend with winter weather, steep terrain, challenging cuts and fills, rock slides, the need to minimize visual and environmental damage, and other perilous working conditions.

In 1931–1932, engineers and construction workers bored Marys Rock tunnel through 670 feet of solid granite at an altitude of 3,514 feet. It was only about an eighth as long as the 5,613-foot Zion-Mt. Carmel tunnel that had opened in Zion National Park two years earlier, or the 4,263-foot tunnel that had been cut beneath Rockfish Gap as early as the 1850s, but local news accounts of its construction attracted a fasci-nated audience. In January 1932, the passageway broke through at the north portal (mile 32.2) to meet the already graded road, and a week later the first cars passed through. Some curious visitors walked a mile from Panorama to see the south portal.

Cars were first officially temporarily allowed on the road on October 23, 1932, only fourteen months after construction began. An additional section of Skyline Drive was not begun for nearly three years (IIA on March 20, 1934), but President Roosevelt's Civilian Conservation Corps began infrastructural and cosmetic work on the completed sections in mid-May 1933. The final section was completed in August 1939.

WHAT YOU SEE NOW: THE DESIGN OF SKYLINE DRIVE

Lin Cove Viaduct on Blue Ridge Parkway. The National Park-to-Park Highway Association was formed in 1916 to promote auto touring in the national parks. The authorization of the Blue Ridge Parkway came quickly on the heels of Shenandoah and Great Smoky Mountains with the vision of connecting the two new eastern parks. *NPS/Blue Ridge Parkway staff*

The Skyline Drive motorists encounter now, so many decades since its construction, appears to be "naturally" and unobtrusively placed, beautifully blended into the surrounding landscape. Engaging vistas appear in sequence on both sides; elevations rise and fall gently; curves sweep manageably; stone walls protect without intruding; barely noticeable stone gutters carry rainwater away and keep the road dry.

Herein lies the central paradox of Skyline Drive's design and construction: it appears to be so "natural," but it was all meticulously planned—from the initial centerline survey down to the last stone and

Severe erosion issues could not be completely addressed until after 1935, when the ownership of the land adjacent to the Skyline Drive's one-hundred-foot right-of-way was transferred to the government. *NPS Archives*

Marys Rock Tunnel was built partly to avoid rockslides, but although not common, they still happened, this one in 1941. *NPS Archives*

post. The engineers and landscape designers who planned the road and oversaw its construction by private contractors left virtually nothing to chance. Dirt from cuts went into nearby fills; stone blasted out of the Marys Rock tunnel went into walls and gutters; native vegetation was disturbed as little as possible, and if new trees and plants were needed for a certain vista, native ones were moved from nearby.

Complicating the process further was the fact that engineers and designers did not always agree—either among themselves or with each other—about every aspect of design and construction, so that much had to be carefully negotiated. Where should the centerline be at any point? How short could the radius of a particular curve safely be? What was the best angle for a slope at any given location? How should stone be placed on an embankment or laid in a wall to produce both stability and the best visual effect? And if, despite all the forethought, planning, and effort, boulders slide into the roadway or an embankment collapses, *then* what?

Overlooks and parking areas presented their own special challenges. None were available when the first section (Panorama to Swift Run Gap) opened, but designs for later sections included them. Early visitors who wanted to see Jewell Hollow, for example, as many did, needed a place to park. But where? North of the vista, or south of it? Which would be most convenient and attractive? Least disturbing of native vegetation? Require the least grading and slope stabilization? Best regulate traffic flow? And how many cars might be expected at any one time? There was no one best answer to all these questions, but a choice had to be made: Jewell Hollow Overlook lies to the south of

Looking North from Jewell Hollow Overlook on Skyline Drive in Shenandoah National Park, Va.

Jewell Hollow Overlook is still a favorite stop for motorists today. *NPS Archives; Publisher Shenandoah Valley News Co., Inc., Winchester, VA; Staley & Staley*

the vista, and is larger than later proved sufficient at other points.

Even guard walls and rails needed (and got) extended discussion—partly, like every other aspect of construction, because selecting one design over another could raise or lower costs dramatically. Wooden guide rails were fairly cheap (especially if made of blighted chestnut trees, which were plentiful) and reasonably durable. Masonry was even more durable, but also more expensive, especially if it was dry-laid, which required more experienced (thus more highly paid) masons.

Whether to pave the road, including (or not) overlooks and picnic grounds parking areas, was debated at length, but by the time the entire Skyline Drive was completed in 1939, it had all been given a durable hard surface.

The costs, aesthetics, and practicalities of all of these options and choices were negotiated at length. Plans and standards continually evolved during the eight years the road was under construction, and the results of choices made at various points (and times) are still in evidence.

Who Constructed Skyline Drive?

Contrary to a widespread misconception, neither Skyline Drive nor the Blue Ridge Parkway was constructed either by hand labor or by the Civilian Conservation Corps (CCC). Both were built by private contractors using standard road construction machinery and techniques of the period. During the nine years (1933–1942) the CCC existed, however, it did supply labor to finish grading cuts and fills, construct water supply and drainage systems, landscape overlooks and recreation areas, and build guard rails and trails.

Chapter V

CCC BOYS: THE CIVILIAN CONSERVATION CORPS

Among all of the New Deal acronyms (AAA, TVA, FERA, WPA, FSA, and many others), the Civilian Conservation Corps (CCC) probably still inspires the most nostalgic affection and pride. Each September, the remaining Shenandoah National Park "CCC boys" and their families return, still glad for having had the CCC opportunity, still proud of the scenic roadway and park they helped to build.

THE NEW DEAL AND THE CCC

The CCC was an early and remarkably productive effort of Franklin D. Roosevelt's New Deal. By 1932, thirteen million people—a quarter of the entire workforce—were out of work, blue-collar workers' wages had fallen by nearly a third, and nearly four out of every ten banks had failed. In much of the Midwest and South, a severe drought brought additional misery. Virginia farmers were hard hit.

CCC insignia pins, modeled after the military, decorated enrollees' and officers' uniforms. *NPS Archives*

President Hoover, whose term didn't end until March 1933, insisted that most of the needed relief should come from states, local jurisdictions, and private charities. President Roosevelt's approach was dramatically different: the federal government itself had to respond, massively and quickly.

During his famous first hundred days, FDR enacted new banking legislation, addressed farm families' distress with new federal agencies, spurred industrial recovery through the National Industrial Recovery Administration (NIRA), created the Tennessee Valley Authority (TVA) to approach regional flood control and redevelopment, channeled $500 million in relief money to the states through the Federal Emergency Relief Administration (FERA), and gave $3.3 billion to the Public Works Administration to give people jobs building roads, dams, schools, hospitals, and other public facilities. During the next decade, FERA's Civil Works Administration (CWA) spent $11 billion employing eight million workers.

Most directly important for Skyline Drive and the projected national park was Roosevelt's Executive Order 6101 of April 5, 1933, establishing the Emergency Conservation Work (ECW) agency (renamed the Civilian Conservation Corps in 1937). Based in part on Roosevelt's prior experience in dealing with reforestation as governor of New York, at first ECW was envisioned as a two-year program to hire 250,000 men to work in national parks and forests, as well as in developing state parks.

By July 1, 1933, there were 172 camps in thirty-five states, and 34,000 youth were at work. The original target of 250,000 enrollees was achieved during the program's first three months, partly because congressmen sought them so intensely for their Depression-plagued districts. At its peak in August 1935, CCC was serving more than 500,000 young men in nearly 3,000 camps, and the press was overwhelmingly supportive. Unemployed men liked the jobs, their families liked the money they sent home, and local merchants liked for the money to circulate.

By the time it was shut down in mid-1942, CCC had served more than two million men (about 5 percent of the male population) and channeled $2.5 billion into the economy.

THE CCC COMES TO SKYLINE DRIVE AND SHENANDOAH

The CCC program brought large resources of money and manpower to the creation of Skyline Drive and Shenandoah National Park, without which both would have been sorely hindered in their development.

The first two CCC camps operated by the National Park Service anywhere in the country were set up in May 1933 at Skyland (NP-1) and Big Meadows (NP-2). By the end of October, there were six

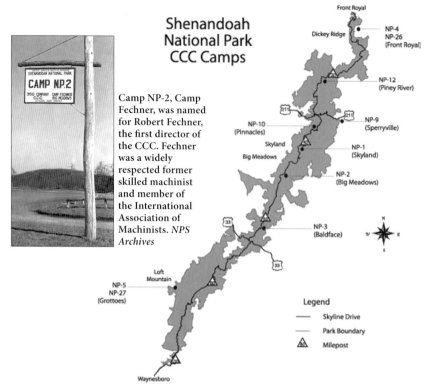

Shenandoah
National Park
CCC Camps

Front Royal

Dickey Ridge

NP-4
NP-26
(Front Royal)

NP-12
(Piney River)

NP-10
(Pinnacles)

NP-9
(Sperryville)

Skyland

Big Meadows

NP-1
(Skyland)

NP-2
(Big Meadows)

NP-3
(Baldface)

Loft
Mountain

NP-5
NP-27
(Grottoes)

Waynesboro

Legend

— Skyline Drive

— Park Boundary

△ Milepost

CAMP NP.2

350 COMPANY CAMP FECHNER
C.C.C.   BIG MEADOWS
NATIONAL PARK SERVICE

Camp NP-2, Camp Fechner, was named for Robert Fechner, the first director of the CCC. Fechner was a widely respected former skilled machinist and member of the International Association of Machinists. *NPS Archives*

camps and 1,200 men, including architects, landscape architects, and engineers to work on Skyline Drive. By late 1940, camps had been added at Baldface (NP-3), Front Royal (NP-4), Grottoes (NP-5), Sperryville (NP-9), Pinnacles (NP-10), Piney River (NP-12), Front Royal (Remount Station; NP-26), and Brown Gap (NP-27). By the time the program ended nine years later, 6,500 men had served in Shenandoah camps.

Not all CCC camps had the luxury of electric lighting, but the barracks at NP-2 did. *NPS Archives*

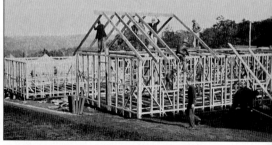

The absence of CCC uniforms suggests that the construction of this barracks at NP-3 in 1933 was done by "Locally Employed Men" (LEMs), probably because the "boys" had not yet acquired the skills needed. *NPS Archives*

As park historian Reed Engle recounts it, the first CCC recruits arrived to find "a ragtag assemblage of World War I surplus tents, field kitchens, and latrines up to two decades old, erected in the middle of muddy cow pastures" and surrounded by countless blight-killed chestnut trees. At the Skyland (NP-1) camp, the first 200 recruits had to cook their meals over outdoor fires until a mess hall could be constructed.

Fortunately, wooden barracks soon replaced the tents, and fully functioning camps came to include mess halls, kitchens, bathhouses, and other equipment, maintenance, and service buildings. The earliest CCC housing was stick-built on-site, but prefabricated modular panels began to arrive in the spring of 1934.

LIFE IN A CCC CAMP

Waverly Groves, a veteran of NP-2 at Big Meadows (1937–1939), recalled a typical day for a typical (unemployed, unmarried, eighteen to twenty-five years old) CCC boy:

> I was up at 6:00 in the morning. We had muster, then breakfast, then went back to clean up our barracks, made up your bed and so forth, if you hadn't made it up before muster. Then you'd return to go to work at 7:30.... We'd come in at maybe 3:30, quarter to four in the evenings. Put in eight hours a day. After working hours, we'd clean up... shower and change clothes for the evening retreat and evening meal.

Those meals were hardy and plentiful—served hot even at midday if work sites were close enough to permit it. There was, as many a

The boys were required to wear their dress uniforms to meals. *NPS Archives*

President Roosevelt conducted an inspection trip to the proposed Shenandoah National Park and dined at Camp NP-2 at Big Meadows. *NPS Archives*

Above: Boxing was another popular sport; medals were awarded along with bragging rights. *NPS Archives*

Top right: The recreation program evolved over the years and held inter-camp competitions in many sports, including basketball. *NPS Archives*

Bottom right: Proceeds from the camp stores financed recreation hall amenities such as billiards tables. *NPS Archives*

CCC boy has recalled, "good wholesome food and plenty of it": eggs, bacon, milk, cereal, and sausage or bacon for breakfast; and chicken, steak, bread, mashed potatoes and gravy, milk, and maybe ice cream for dinner (at which dress uniforms were required).

Groves's account of a typical CCC camp day suggests the general outline of CCC camp life, but the boys' days also included sports activities (baseball, basketball, boxing, football, swimming, and track). Some sports events took place in gymnasiums built by CCC boys in their off hours. CCC teams competed against each other, or sometimes against those from local high schools or military bases. Most camps also had a small library.

Educational programs in CCC camps were few during the early months, but became more numerous as the program developed. Out-of-work teachers assigned to the camps taught basic education classes as well as radio, music, woodworking, and journalism (the latter published camp newspapers). Numerous musical groups formed, and visitors from local towns frequently attended CCC dances. On outings to Luray, Stanley, Front Royal, Sperryville, or other nearby towns, CCC boys sought (of course) the companionship of young ladies, not a few of whom they

Sweetheart pins were among the keepsakes boys could purchase from the camp store. *NPS Archives*

Impromptu groups formed among the boys interested in music. *NPS Archives*

married. Waverly Groves was one of three CCC boys who courted and married one of the Painter sisters from Stanley.

Health care in the camps was necessarily rudimentary, but readily available in the camp's military field hospital, staffed by an army doctor or medic. In those

Dancing lessons prepared the boys for trips into town and the occasional camp dance when local girls were bused in. *NPS Archives*

pre-antibiotic days, a small cut or scratch could lead to fatal blood poisoning, and social diseases (not uncommon) were the subject of frequent precautionary lectures.

TREES, SHELTERS, RAILS, AND GUTTERS: THE CCC AT WORK

Construction of Skyline Drive had been under way for nearly two years before the CCC arrived in May 1933, and there was as yet no Shenandoah National Park. Skyline Drive itself (not to become part of the new park for another two and a half years) had such a narrow right-of-way (one hundred feet, bordered by privately owned land) that it offered only limited opportunities for CCC work.

Nevertheless, there was plenty of work to be done, and every morning at 7:30, crews set off for their work sites. A great deal of the work they did during their first months focused on landscaping Skyline Drive. Some worked with contractors' crews, shaping and landscaping slopes as the crews moved forward. Others removed trees and shrubs that obscured desired views, transplanted others to enhance roadsides and overlooks, built guard walls and drainage systems, and laid electrical cable.

Each morning work crews piled on trucks to be transported to work sites throughout the park. *NPS Archives*

CCC boys shaped and landscaped construction scars left by grading contractors. *NPS Archives*

Many visitors to Shenandoah don't realize that the beautiful laurel that blooms in profusion along Skyline Drive in early June was planted by CCC boys. *Library of Congress*

During the years the CCC boys worked in Shenandoah, they transplanted thousands of trees. *NPS Archives*

After development of Shenandoah National Park began in January 1936, CCC workers branched out into additional activities, including building construction. Several buildings, including a CCC administration building, were built at Piney River. A splendid shelter they built at Pinnacles (mile 36.7) is still in use, as is the beautiful stone Park Headquarters building on U.S. Highway 211.

On the whole, the CCC effort met with great public enthusiasm, and was managed efficiently and effectively. Hundreds of thousands of young men from all over the country flocked to the camps, forwarding most of their modest incomes back home to help families in need. Interviewed years later, former CCC boys spoke with pride about what they had done, and what happened to them in the process. "CCC was one of the best things that's ever happened," recalled John Shuda, who spent nearly five years in Camp NP-12 at Piney River. "Not only to my life, [but] to many men's lives."

The infrastructure needed to ready the park for visitors, such as laying electrical cable, was created by the work of the CCC. *Library of Congress*

The CCC's work was not confined to national forests and parks. They also helped build and develop nearly three million acres for 800 state parks in forty-one states— eight of them in Virginia (Douthat, Westmoreland, Pocahontas, Hungry Mother, Fairy Stone, Staunton River, Seashore [later First Landing], and Prince William).

In Shenandoah National Park, however, the legacy of the CCC is still much in evidence in stone walls and guard rails and gutters; graded and landscaped slopes and fills on Skyline Drive; trails and campgrounds; picnic and parking areas; and the remaining CCC buildings and shelters. Fittingly, a statue commemorating the CCC boys and their work stands prominently at the entrance to Byrd Visitor Center.

Top: The beauty and craftsmanship in the stone and woodwork in Park Headquarters is a testament to the CCC. *NPS Archives*

Bottom: The CCC-built picnic shelter at Pinnacles (mile 36.7) is still enjoyed by visitors today. *Library of Congress*

The "Iron Mike" statue graces many of the former CCC work sites throughout the country. This one at Shenandoah was donated by a former enrollee's family to commemorate the importance of the program in his life. *NPS/Ed Knepley*

Chapter VI

The Farm Security Administration hired photographer Arthur Rothstein to document the lives of those being relocated by the establishment of the park. He took this photo of Russ Nicholson in 1935. *Library of Congress*

Acquiring land for large national parks in the East presented a special challenge: what to do about the thousands of people who had long made their homes and built their communities on those lands? Move them all out? Let them stay? Let some stay in certain areas or under certain conditions?

And what about the monuments to their labor left on the land: the gardens, orchards, pastures, houses, fences, walls, and barns? Who could calculate their value, and by what measures?

Early in November of 1935, Richard Nicholson, whose house and land were being taken, wrote from his home near Skyland to J. R. Lassiter, later the first superintendent of the park but then managing preparatory work for the removals. "My Dear Sir," Nicholson began,

> I am writing you to see if you will give me permission to cut some dry wood [from parkland] and sell it by the cord.... I would be very glad and thankful to you if you would let me cut the wood. As I dont have any employment of no kind.... Of course if it is against the rule I would not want to cut it. My father is dead and I am the only one to look after my mother. Please do what you can for me as I am in tough luck for the winter.
>
> My mother and I thank you for letting us stay and we want to obey park Rules.

Nicholson's dilemma was shared by many: the park was coming, and at this late date there was no way to stop it. His house and land lay within the boundary. The new rules had to be obeyed, and those rules said he had to move. It would probably be more productive to address the new authorities with respect than to antagonize them. But how was one to feed one's family or take care of aging parents without any way to make a living?

By the time Mr. Nicholson wrote his letter, plans for the park had been under way for more than a decade, and numerous people had cautioned that moving hundreds of people out might cause trouble. As early as February 1925, Skyland Resort owner George Freeman Pollock assured local people that if and when it was created,

> ...you will probably not have to leave the farm which you sold the government.... You are not going to have anything taken away from you in the long run, but you are going to have a great deal provided for you by Uncle Sam.

Even as late as December 1933, L. Ferdinand Zerkel, who had worked for years to bring the park into being, wrote to his colleague William Carson that "Any 'wholesale'... group removal would... be very unpopular and prove later to have been ill-advised."

Nevertheless, Park Service Director Arno B. Cammerer, asserting that "there is no person so canny as certain types of mountaineers, and none so disreputable," decided in February 1934 that "all inhabitants of the park lands... [will] have to leave." Population removal thus became official policy. But Zerkel's fears proved well founded: distrust, ill

A stone wall and blooming irises are still visible on the Snead family farm in the park's northern district. *NPS/Robert Kuhns*

will, and conflict over that policy emerged immediately and continued for decades.

Along with the many wonderful stories associated with the park's history, the story of the removals also needs to be told. Why was such a policy adopted? How was it implemented, and with what results—both initially and through the years? Who objected, how, and with what results? And how has the park itself dealt with that part of its history?

THE "HOLLOW FOLK" MOMENT

In the mid-1930s, removal seemed acceptable partly because there were precedents for it: the Park Service had removed Native Americans from some western parks, the Tennessee Valley Authority was clearing people and communities from reservoir sites up and down the rivers, and removals from the new Great Smoky Mountains National Park (most notably in Cades Cove and Cataloochee, but elsewhere as well) were well advanced.

Both Shenandoah and the Great Smokies parks were also planned as "nature" parks, oriented toward the revitalization of lands damaged by logging and other uses, and toward their leisure use by eastern urban dwellers.

New parks in the Great Smokies and the Blue Ridge were authorized at the same time, but after John D. Rockefeller, Jr. made a $5-million gift for land acquisition in the Great Smokies, land-buying proceeded quickly there, and conflicts over removals arose early.

In the Blue Ridge, where no such funds were available, and many hundreds of people lived within the initial 521,000-acre boundary (later much reduced), officials moved more slowly, hoping to avoid conflict. But lawsuits filed early by some landowners made a wholly peaceful process unlikely.

Scientific documentation became available, it appeared, in *The Hollow Folk* (1933) by University of Chicago psychologist Mandel Sherman and journalist Thomas R. Henry. Guided to supposedly representative study areas by Skyland owner George Freeman Pollock, provided data by field workers Miriam Sizer and Minnie Meyer, and supported with funds from professional research organizations, Sherman and Henry produced what was widely accepted (at the time and for many years thereafter) as an authoritative analysis of five mountain ("hollow") communities.

As described by Sherman and Henry, the communities could as easily have been Li'l Abner and Daisy Mae's Dogpatch. "The dark interior valleys of the Blue Ridge," they wrote, "are realms of enchantment."

> Here, hidden in deep mountain pockets, dwell families of unlettered folk, of almost pure Anglo-Saxon stock, sheltered in tiny, mud-plastered log cabins and supported by a primitive agriculture.

These hollow folk, readers were told, lacked government, religion, social organization, and industry. Their ragged children had never seen the flag, didn't know the Lord's Prayer, and had never heard of President Hoover. Most hollow dwellers couldn't read, marriages were informal, schools were few and the school year brief, houses were unkempt, and prostitution common. Conditions in some places were a bit better than in others, but the trend, readers were given to understand, was downward. It was a case of "the decline of human culture."

Popular reaction to *The Hollow Folk* was mostly positive (and credulous). The *Boston Transcript* judged (March 18, 1933) that Sherman and Henry presented their findings "without bias... in an easy, conversational style... in spite of the sordid scenes and pitiable peoples revealed."

The next day, a *New York Times* reviewer called the Blue Ridge hollows "a leprous spot in our national body." The book's pages fascinate, he said, "because the conditions they disclose of squalor, of stupidity, of degradation, of deterioration to a point that comes near to being lower than the human type are so appalling as to be almost unbelievable."

Reviews in popular journals were mixed. *Survey Midmonthly* (May 1933) found this supposed "record of [the mountaineers'] culture" to be "as near perhaps to the laboratory experiment as is possible." But *The New Republic* (November 1933) only commented blandly that the book was "full of interesting detail" about the "lives and customs" of a group "isolated from practically all civilized contacts for over a century."

The consensus was, in any case, that Sherman and Henry had it about right: these Blue Ridge hollow dwellers ought—both for their own good and for that of the park—to be moved out to where they could live better, learn more, salute the flag, and say the Lord's Prayer.

This portrayal of the residents of the Blue Ridge, while embraced by the popular media of the time, would prove to be problematic for decades.

REMOVAL AND RESETTLEMENT

Moving nearly 500 families out of the park proved to be (as Zerkel and others had feared) a messy, prolonged, and conflicted process. Some went willingly, some sued, some resisted physically until they were forcibly removed. Special exceptions were made for about forty "aged and especially meritorious" people, who were allowed to remain on their land as long as they lived. The last of them to die (at ninety-two) was Annie Shenk, who lived until 1979.

Many residents who had been told they had to move wrote letters to park managers, seeking small concessions that might ease the burden of the transition. Some merely asked to stay long enough to make a garden; others asked to dismantle and take wood from old buildings that were going to be torn down anyway. Elizabeth Seal wanted to harvest her apples; James Ramey wanted to salvage building and roofing materials; Ambrose Shiflett and others wanted to take old barbed wire fencing; W. D. Taylor and C. M. Good wanted to collect dead wood; and Charles Melton wanted to salvage some fence rails. Robert Matthews of Bentonville wrote Superintendent Lassiter "about the hay on the place in wich I lived I think it is a bad thing to sea it all go to wast as bad as I need it and as much work as I did on it last year."

Careful observers will find bits of fencing and old posts throughout the park. *NPS/Mara Meisel*

Flint Hill was among the seven homestead communities created by the Resettlement Administration for qualifying families. *Library of Congress*

Some families were able to locate new land and homes on their own, but others received assistance from the federal government through a homesteading project. Beginning in October 1937, 172 families were moved into one of seven homesteading sites in Greene, Madison, Rappahannock, and Rockingham counties. Relocations were not completed until 1938.

Once the residents were gone, Superintendent James Lassiter moved quickly to tear down and burn many houses and other structures in order to return the land to its "natural" state.

Newly homesteaded residents reacted in a variety of ways to their new homes. Some liked them and stayed for a long time; others did not, and moved on as soon as they could. Many had mixed feelings. Virginia's senator Harry Byrd, a very vocal opponent of the New Deal, called the project "communistic" and scoffed that the mountain people had no need for indoor privies

Late fall and winter, when the leaves have fallen, reveal many vestiges of former residents. *NPS/Mara Meisel*

or other trappings of modern life. Partisans and officials of the New Deal, on the other hand, were proud of what they had accomplished.

Many residents never got over their pain, or let go of the hope that someday they might go back. Ten years after he wrote to ask Lassiter's

Some of the resettlement communities were more successful than others. Ida Valley and Flint Hill boasted some long-term success while not a single home in the Greene County settlement was ever purchased by a park family. *Library of Congress*

Most homesteads included a modest home with indoor plumbing, a small barn, and at least enough land for a garden. *Library of Congress*

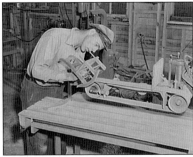

The Ida Valley homestead community was built in the shadow of the residents' former homes. The resettled families were to pay five dollars per month in the first year and then were expected to purchase the homestead at appraised values with as much as forty years to pay. *Library of Congress*

The Resettlement Administration promoted mountain crafts and skills as a way for the former residents to earn income sufficient to make their mortgage payments on their new homes. *Library of Congress*

permission to cut and sell cord wood, Richard Nicholson asked Senator Byrd if there was any chance he and others could get their homes back. The mountain people "was badly misled," he said, "when they sold their land for a park believing that they could stay there and not be forced to move." Nine out of ten of those living in the new homesteads, he reported, "would rather go back to their old home in the mountains. Because they were born and reared in the mountains and they will never be satisfied otherwise."

CHALLENGING THE REMOVALS

Informal letters of petition from individuals about to be moved out of the park were generally polite and deferential, but others chose to file suit or resist in some other formal way.

Landowner Lewis Willis, a University of Virginia graduate, organized a Landowners Protective Association as early as 1929. He and the association held meetings and wrote letters to newspaper editors and public officials, but their efforts to stop the park were unsuccessful. Willis himself was eventually allowed to remain on the sixty acres he sold to the government, but he continued to resist the land-taking for more than twenty-five years, finally as an octogenarian living alone in a house piled with documents from his struggle.

The most complicated and threatening suit was one filed by Robert H. Via in November 1934. It reached the Supreme Court before being dismissed in late 1935, clearing the way for the government to acquire clear title to the parklands.

As late as the 1990s, a group of descendents of families removed from the park more than a half-century earlier formed Children of the Shenandoah (COS) to publicize their longstanding complaints about the park's failure to incorporate the story of the removals into its exhibits and preservation efforts. Committed "to preserving the heritage and culture of our forefathers who once lived contented, productive and undisturbed on the land that is now The Shenandoah National Park," they were determined to see that "presentations of our people... are historically accurate and do not omit personal losses and dehumanization suffered through the creation of the Park."

Achieving the latter goal took years of work by both COS and the park. In the mid-1990s, the park opened serious dialog with removal descendents, and engaged in an energetic and sustained effort to redress their grievances, remove misleading exhibits, and rework the park's interpretation of the removals.

In early 2000, park officials began cataloging the archive and preparing a new archives facility, but lack of staff and funds curtailed the effort. Some descendents suspected that the delay might be motivated by an effort to restrict what could be written and who could write it. Park officials denied that that was the case, and scholar Katrina Powell was allowed brief access (2000–2003) to several hundred letters about the removals, on which she subsequently based two books that strongly reinforced descendents' concerns.

Other efforts went back not to the written record, but to the physical record of the families who had been removed.

REVISITING THE HOLLOW FOLK

In 1995, the National Park Service collaborated with the Colonial Williamsburg Foundation on the Survey of Rural Mountain Settlement. Conducted by anthropologist Audrey Horning, the survey (1995–1998) focused on Corbin, Nicholson, and Weakley hollows—the subject of *The Hollow Folk* sixty-two years earlier.

Horning located eighty-eight significant archeological sites covering 2,500 acres. Investigating fifteen of them, she found abundant

A decorative glass touring car, 75 rpm fragments of records, a toy truck, and the remnants of a ceramic dish, all archeological finds in the park, belie the claim of "isolated residents." *NPS Archives*

evidence that people in three of the hollows (Corbin, Weakley, and Nicholson) owned and used virtually the same array of objects used by families elsewhere.

Augmenting her archeological investigations with courthouse documents, interviews with "Children of the Shenandoah," and other public records, Horning easily established that "hollow folk"—who according to Sherman and Henry were illiterate "squatters" who owned no land and left no records—"were buying and selling their lands, paying taxes, filing wills, and occasionally taking disputes to court...."

The three hollows themselves were in fact quite different, Horning showed—not because, as *The Hollow Folk* authors argued, each happened to occupy a different position on the slippery slope of general cultural decline or to have made a bad choice of ancestors, but primarily because their topographies and resources (and thus their histories) were different.

Lowest on the slope, the "poster child" of the *Hollow Folk* campaign, was Corbin Hollow, characterized in a 1932 Associated Press report of a visit by Interior Secretary Ray Lyman Wilbur as "a community of perennial starvation and penniless squalor." Settled latest of the three areas, Corbin grew up as a service community for George Freeman Pollock's Stony Man (later Skyland) resort, founded in 1894. Pollock needed cooks and maids and janitors, and the families of Corbin Hollow (where farmable land was scarce)—and from Nicholson Hollow as well—needed work. The mutual dependency became starkly evident when the Depression hit and Corbin Hollow workers had nowhere else to get work. Significantly, that was the moment at which the *Hollow Folk* researchers appeared.

Also discovered during excavations (top), a store-bought "33 Repeater" toy ray gun. On the bottom is a relatively unused version of the popular 1930s toy. *NPS Archives*

Archeologists excavated ceramic dinnerware at the homesite of Charley and Mazie Nicholson. *NPS Archives*

When they had work, Horning's archeological investigations showed, Corbin Hollow residents bought (like anyone else) what they needed at the store or from mail-order catalogs, including costume jewelry, ceramic dinnerware, porcelain dolls, baseballs, harmonicas, and phonograph records for family entertainment. Incomprehensibly from the *Hollow Folk* perspective ("nor do they know the meaning of the term toys"), one Corbin Hollow child played happily with a "33 Repeater" toy ray gun made in Wyandotte, Michigan.

A rusting axle and wheels prove that residents were acquiring modern equipment outside of the mountain. *NPS/Mara Meisel*

A widely respected community leader, William Brown was the postmaster and storekeeper at Old Rag. *Library of Congress*

Quite a few of the mountain residents were excellent basketmakers, at first out of the need for baskets and then, even today, as a viable craft industry. *Library of Congress*

Stone chimneys and foundations dot the landscape, reminding visitors of those who sacrificed their homes for the establishment of the park. *NPS/Mara Meisel*

More agricultural Nicholson Hollow had a much longer and more diverse history than Corbin. Some of its families had arrived in the eighteenth century. Through the years, residents had included land speculators, slaveholders and slaves, lumbermen, subsistence farmers, herders, skilled blacksmiths and other artisans, distillers, and (more recently) basketmakers.

The land on the banks of Harrison's Run where Ephraim and Patsy Nicholson raised thirteen children in a twenty-five-by-thirty-foot log house included an orchard of over one hundred fruit trees, a barn and shed, two henhouses, and two corncribs. The family raised corn and grain as well as cattle, and Ephraim, a skilled stonemason, brought in extra income by working at Skyland.

Ephraim and Patsy's son Edward remembered a home filled with the voices of children, music, and laughter. "People would stop by almost every night," he recalled, to make music. Patsy played harmonica, and Edward and his brother played banjo and fiddle (likely bought by mail-order, one surmises).

Far from the pervasive dysfunction and disorder portrayed in *The Hollow Folk*, Horning's work showed, much of the family life in

An abandoned automobile rusts away in the backcountry. *NPS/Mara Meisel*

Nicholson Hollow seems to have been stable, healthy, and enjoyable. Newton and Emily Nicholson's daughter described her own family home as "the sweetest place I was at in my whole life."

Weakley Hollow, unlike almost exclusively agricultural Nicholson, or Skyland-dependent Corbin, had a mixed agricultural and commercial economy.

Indeed, the community was not located in a "hollow" (isolated or not) at all, but rather on rich bottomland. A good road linked the farms, the village of Old Rag, commercial orchards, a school, two churches, and a store that sold Nehi and Coke. The most respected resident, postmaster and community leader William Austin Brown, lived in a six-room log and frame house. Highland Baptist Church pastor Howard Berry and his wife Annie had a seven-room frame house on 120 acres, and an orchard of 150 apple trees.

Clearly, substantial cash was changing hands in Weakley Hollow. Horning's excavations turned up food cans, Coca Cola bottles, baby food jars, 78 rpm record fragments, a medical thermometer, parts of a gold-plated watch, decorative glassware, and Limoges porcelain dish fragments (offered in the 1902 Sears, Roebuck catalog). Sixty years after the removals, other evidence lay scattered across the landscape: fence posts, a swimming pool, chimneys and stone walls, fragments of a cast-iron stove, and the rusted remains of an automobile.

Both new perspectives on the removals and a wealth of new information made it imperative for the park to update its interpretation of the removal, as it began to do in 1995. The effort was funded with park fee receipts, and benefited greatly from the arrival of new staff trained in historical research and exhibit planning.

Guided partly by Audrey Horning's archeological investigations of mid-1990 and extensive conversations with descendents of the removals (including members of Children of the Shenandoah), park staff worked for more than a decade to develop a new $1-million exhibit in Byrd Visitor Center at Big Meadows, which included forthright and engaging sections on both Lewis Mountain and the removals.

The park's broad-gauged effort to reconsider and revamp its treatment of the removals resulted from its determination to interpret responsibly not only the history of the area in which it was situated, but its own history as well.

Real Appalachia

To understand the history and culture of Appalachia, one can best begin by setting aside the common notions that Appalachia was ever isolated, homogeneously rural (or anything else), or static.

Shenandoah National Park historian Darwin Lambert's discussion of trade routes through the Blue Ridge makes clear that the area where the park now is was never isolated. The headwaters of the Rappahannock reached back toward Front Royal, and a road through Thornton Gap to Luray (now U.S. Highway 211) was already so heavily used by 1786 that it had to be improved. A few miles to the south, a military road stretched across the ridge from Criglersville toward Stanley. Further south, the so-called Spotswood Trail ran from Stanardsville across the mountain to Elkton, and near the southern end of what is now the park ran Brown Gap Road from Mechum to Grottoes.

Between the military road and Spotswood Trail, the headwaters of the Rapidan drained the slopes before joining the Rappahannock, coming out of Chester Gap near Front Royal and flowing to the coast. On the rivers and over the roads passed endless shipments of farm products, textiles and clothing, iron and copper ore, tools and manufactured hardware, rum and bourbon.

The Weakley family musicians entertained visitors at overlooks along Skyline Drive. *NPS Archives*

As the goods flowed, so did culture: the songs people sang and the instruments they played them on, the languages and dialects they spoke, the recipes they cherished, the religious beliefs and practices that guided them.

These cultural elements were far from static, however. They came in (later than is generally thought), mixed and mingled, and produced new hybrid forms and traditions. The banjo that is usually assumed to have "always" been in the mountains was of African origin, and was rare in the southern mountains until after the Civil War. The guitar came a few years later, mostly from the Sears, Roebuck catalog. What we now call "old time gospel" emerged toward the end of the nineteenth century (spurred partly by inexpensive song books published by such companies as the Shenandoah Valley's Ruebush-Kieffer Company), and bluegrass music didn't appear until the mid-1940s.

Again contradicting the popular myth of Appalachia as non-urban and non-industrialized, the cities we now know as the region's larger ones began to appear by the end of the eighteenth century: Wheeling, West Virginia (1782); Knoxville, Tennessee (1786); Asheville, North Carolina (1794); and Charleston, West Virginia (1794). Chattanooga, Tennessee (1838), and many others followed in the nineteenth century.

Industrialization also arrived early and became widespread: salt works to Charleston, West Virginia, in 1797 and steamboats in the 1820s; copper mines to Virginia, North Carolina, and Tennessee after 1832; ironworks to Scranton in 1840; cart and coach making to Greenville, South Carolina, in the 1850s; railroads to Roanoke in 1852; industrial-scale coal mines from the 1870s onward; and chemical plants around Asheville and Charleston after World War I.

As industry arrived, so did wage labor—frequently at wages that were not very good. To get those jobs, many people had to move off the farms and into cities, towns, coal camps, and cotton mill towns, where they were as likely to mingle with new immigrant workers as with former neighbors. Nearly overnight, towns could appear, double or triple their populations, or (later) die and be abandoned as forests fell beneath the axe, coal seams were mined out, or mills moved elsewhere in search of cheaper labor.

Finally, people who lived in the mountains have never been (as is usually assumed) all white or all Protestant. Virtually every county in the region (however defined) had slaves, blacks came in great numbers to work in the mines, and virtually all towns and cities (like Luray, for example, or Asheville, or Chattanooga, or Roanoke) have had significant black populations. Wheeling, West Virginia, had a Catholic diocese by 1815, and by the 1990s, the region counted nearly a quarter-million Catholics. Appalachia has also had Jewish congregations at least since the 1840s.

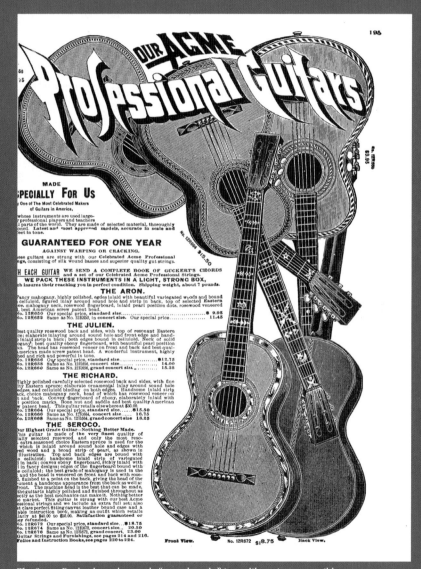

The Sears, Roebuck catalog made "store-bought" items like guitars accessible.

Chapter VII

"LAWS AND GENERALLY ACCEPTED CUSTOMS": RACE AND CULTURE AT LEWIS MOUNTAIN

Several miles north of where Skyline Drive crosses Highway 33 stands a familiar brown Park Service sign directing travelers to the Lewis Mountain picnicking and camping area. Driving across the small rise that separates the area from the road, one sees cabins, camp sites arranged around loop drives, picnic tables, family tents, and children riding bicycles. Nothing out of the ordinary.

Everything looks as if it could have been here since the early 1940s, as indeed much of it has been. To the right is a camp store, but the building wasn't always a store. Therein lies one of the more complicated (and conflicted) stories in Shenandoah National Park's history.

The Lewis Mountain story lies beyond today's directional sign. *NPS/Norman Forder*

Luray native Beulah Billings knew that story because she worked at Lewis Mountain. Reminiscing during the summer of 2007, Billings remembered the store when it was a lodge with a large stone fireplace. She worked there because Virginia Sky-Line Company, the park's concessionaire, preferred to hire blacks for an area that was, as a very different sign advised then, a "Negro Area."

Although overt segregation ended fairly soon after the park's establishment with the removal of signs like this one, real desegregation of the park's facilities was a long time coming. *NPS Archives*

The Lewis Mountain story reminds us that some park landscapes result from layered histories that repay a closer look. Indeed, the small rise one had to cross to get into Lewis Mountain was put there so that white travelers in the 1940s would not be upset by the sight of blacks using the park. On the far side of that rise lie remnants of a story worth knowing.

THE RACIAL MOMENT

Fortunately, it has been decades since signs warned that this or that motel, bus seat, drinking fountain, or school was for whites or blacks only. Overtly racist cartoons disappeared long ago from local newspapers, and more recent images of fire hoses and dogs, freedom marches, and school boycotts have softened in our memories. Not all of the nation's racial problems have been solved, but progress has been steady and real.

Time, distance, and change carry a risk, however. We may by now have lost some of the perspective we need in order to understand Lewis Mountain—a perspective not only local but national; not limited just to the 1930s, but extending forward and back in time as well.

Looking outward from Lewis Mountain, one is mindful first of the Commonwealth of Virginia, which had passed its earliest race-based laws by 1650, and continued to elaborate them for more than 275 years. At the time Shenandoah National Park began to be developed, Virginia Senator Harry F. Byrd was a staunch segregationist and his colleague Carter Glass openly advocated disenfranchising black voters.

Page County and Luray fit the national mold closely. Black residents could live only in West Luray; black businesses were concentrated in an area called "The Hill." On into the 1960s, everything remained segregated; Luray's last all-black school closed in 1966, a dozen years after *Brown v. Board of Education*. Not far down the road, Prince Edward County closed its public schools for five years (1959–1964) rather than integrate them. Following the "massive resistance" policy championed by Virginia Senator (and Shenandoah advocate) Harry F. Byrd, schools were also shut down in Front Royal, Norfolk, and Charlottesville.

Socially, economically, politically, and culturally, then, the patterns of racism into which Shenandoah National Park was born in 1936 had deep and stubborn roots that stretched all across the country. Not surprisingly, neither the National Park Service nor the New Deal itself was immune.

"COLORED CAMPING GROUNDS": THE NEW DEAL, THE PARK SERVICE, AND A NEW PARK

When Franklin D. Roosevelt was elected in 1932, southern congressmen chaired two-thirds of the most important committees in the Congress. Many used their power to block or dilute civil rights legislation.

Because he needed their votes, President Roosevelt allowed the "Dixie bloc" to have effective veto power over New Deal programs, stripping them of features that did not "respect" established racial boundaries and customs. Virginia senators Byrd and Glass, says Lewis Mountain historian Ellen Krutko, "viewed the New Deal as a threat to their economic and social conservatism, their racial views, their... belief in class privilege, and their... control of the folks back home."

Historian Eric Foner observed that Roosevelt himself "seems to have had little personal interest in race relations or civil rights," and that to many blacks the New Deal demonstrated how strong a hold racial inequality had on public policy.

It was not a surprise, then, that blacks benefited less from New Deal programs than whites. Social Security excluded agricultural and domestic workers, many of whom were black. The Agricultural Adjustment Administration's cotton price support program drove tens of thousands of black sharecroppers off the land, and the Federal Housing Administration channeled its mortgage money into segregated communities. Later critics of the New Deal charged that the National Recovery Administration (NRA) actually created incentives for white racists to discriminate against low-wage black labor.

This culture of racism within New Deal agencies extended to the Department of the Interior, which housed the National Park Service. Even though his predecessor had tried to desegregate the Department of the Interior, and even though he himself held progressive views on race (he invited the African American soprano Marian Anderson to perform in front of the Lincoln Memorial on the Mall in 1939), New Deal Interior Secretary Harold Ickes inherited an agency that proved difficult and slow to change.

The price of locating a new national park in Virginia, it turned out, was an agreement to abide by the state's stringently racist laws and "generally accepted customs." Three years before Shenandoah National Park was officially established, NPS official Arno B. Cammerer instructed that "provision for colored guests" would have to be made. After his promotion to director, Cammerer decreed in September 1936 that "separate facilities for white and colored people... [are] necessary to conform with the generally accepted customs long established in Virginia.... [Hence] separate rest rooms, cabin colonies and picnic ground[s]... should be provided." Cammerer's superior Ickes backed him up by saying that "colored camping grounds" and "picnic places" would have to be developed forthwith, even though this directive contradicted his well-known personal convictions.

Thus the "separate but equal" requirement was written into Shenandoah National Park's operating plan from the beginning. But the decision proved difficult either to implement or to change. NPS Associate Director Arthur Demaray cautioned that the policy was not to operate "to such an extent as to interfere with the complete enjoyment of the park equally by all alike," but that proved much easier said than done.

ON THE ONE HAND (AND ON THE OTHER): PUTTING "SEPARATE BUT EQUAL" INTO PLACE

Following NPS policy, the park's summer 1937 contract with park concessionaire Virginia Sky-Line Company included a "colored picnic grounds" at Lewis Mountain. The Park Service wanted the company to develop the area quickly, but the facility did not open during that summer. Some work had been done by the following summer, but a second such facility planned for further south at Jenkins Gap was never begun.

Even before Lewis Mountain opened, the separate but equal policy had come under widespread criticism. Some Interior Department lawyers were telling Secretary Ickes that it was unwise (and probably unconstitutional) to create separate facilities, and that the federal government was not bound by the "laws and customs of Virginia." The Interior Department's adviser on Negro affairs also wanted "separate but equal" ended eventually, but cautioned Ickes to move carefully.

Lewis Mountain picnic grounds hosted many church and family picnics. *NPS Archives*

After much wrangling, the park's concessionaire during its early years, Virginia Sky-Line, finally opened three overnight cabins at Lewis Mountain in July of 1940. *Library of Congress*

Meanwhile, Virginia Sky-Line feared that it would lose money because there was "no demand" for such facilities. Park Superintendent James Lassiter insisted that already available facilities for whites and blacks were equal, even though as late as the winter of 1939 the Lewis Mountain area still had no lodge, overnight cabins, picnic areas, or comfort stations.

Tired of the wrangling, Secretary Ickes in February 1939 asked senators Byrd and Glass what they thought about just ending segregation in the park altogether. Byrd said he had heard no complaints of injustice, and reminded Ickes that the agreement to create the park included a promise to abide by all state laws.

Faced with such dissension, Ickes remained cautious. The park would "generally" follow state laws and customs, he directed, but Virginia Sky-Line had to provide facilities for blacks that were really equal. Signs referring to racial separation had to be taken down, and one existing picnic area (Pinnacles) was to be designated for black as well as white use. Black picnickers and motorists were also allowed to use the far corners (only) of the South River and Elk Wallow picnic grounds.

In the spring of 1939, Virginia Sky-Line agreed to provide additional dining rooms for blacks at Lewis Mountain, Panorama, and Swift Run Gap. Dickey Ridge, Skyland, and Big Meadows dining rooms would remain white only, but lunch counters could serve blacks. The Lewis

Mountain development was rushed to completion in mid-1940—partly, according to NPS Director Cammerer, as "an insurance policy against future excessive demands for installations for Negroes."

"THE JOINT WAS JUMPIN'": LEWIS MOUNTAIN AS A "NEGROES ONLY" AREA

Not surprisingly, blacks were not pleased with such ambivalent and contradictory arrangements. Negotiations about what exactly Lewis Mountain was going to be, how and by whom it would be used, and how segregated Shenandoah National Park would remain continued for years.

Since recreational areas and overnight accommodations for blacks were scarce outside the park, however, Lewis Mountain came to be a major gathering and recreational space for both local people and travelers from elsewhere. Virginia Sky-Line hired African American workers and managers from the local area, and the managers in turn tended to hire their young relatives.

Amelia and/or Lloyd Tutt worked at Lewis Mountain as managers for twelve years. In a 1978 interview, Lloyd Tutt (World War II veteran, mechanic, and former cook at President Hoover's Rapidan Camp) recalled that he had been instructed to tell white visitors seeking accommodations that the campground was full. He didn't turn anyone away, however, so that the area became unofficially integrated at night. A hot band played boogie woogie on Friday nights, and word had it that the

Lloyd (left) and Amelia "Mittie" (right) Tutt were managers at Lewis Mountain. *NPS Archives*

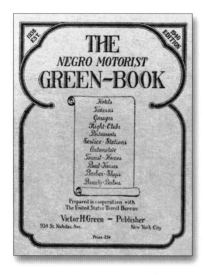

food was better than anywhere else in the park. "The joint was jumpin'," Tutt recalled. "We had a piano and a nickelodeon so there was music and dancing every night. Often entertainers were staying there and so sometimes they sang for us," he remembered. "We had some of the best singers up there. They would come in… and have the biggest jubilee and dances and things that you ever heard of."

Accustomed to having to resort to *The Negro Motorist Green Book* to find restaurants and over-night accommodations, African American travelers embraced Lewis Mountain as an option, arriving in family cars or buses—sometimes as many as 300 at a time. Delicious food served in the main room of the lodge with its large stone fireplace at the end, together with excellent service, made Lewis Mountain a popular attraction for large numbers of travelers, many of whom returned every year. A couple who owned a newspaper in Kansas City returned repeatedly, as did church and student groups and professional organizations. Romantically inclined local teens seeking to rendezvous unimpeded by parental supervision

An all-black bus tour from Cordoza Night High School arrived to explore Shenandoah. *NPS Archives*

also took advantage of the privacy Lewis Mountain offered. Even after the entire park was desegregated, African American individuals and groups continued to return to Lewis Mountain because they preferred it, and treasured the memories they had made there.

SIGNS VS. FACTS: DESEGREGATING LEWIS MOUNTAIN AND SHENANDOAH NATIONAL PARK

The earliest park signs, maps, and brochures made clear that segregation was the official policy, but they drew many complaints. As objections multiplied, Secretary Ickes ordered the offending maps and brochures withdrawn, but the deeply rooted practice of racial separation was not easily obliterated, especially since the segregation policy and park signs remained unchanged for nearly fifteen years.

Despite repeated protests from the National Association for the Advancement of Colored People (NAACP) and individual visitors, Superintendent Lassiter dismissed complaints as emanating from "a few radicals." He also exaggerated reports of racial incidents in order to emphasize the danger of desegregating park facilities. Rangers even marked new race-neutral maps by hand to show the "Negro" areas, and Lassiter himself called for "more and bigger 'For White Only' signs."

In any case, a January 1941 NPS study reported that Negro visitors to Shenandoah accounted for only slightly over 1 percent of the

Facilities in Shenandoah carried signs indicating who could use them. *NPS Archives*

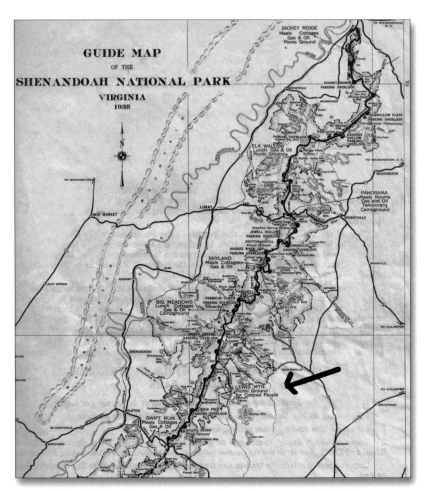

Maps at the entrance stations directed black visitors to Lewis Mountain. *NPS Archives*

total. Except at Lewis Mountain, lodging was available to whites only. Dining rooms for blacks were available only at Lewis Mountain, Panorama, and Swift Run Gap, though lunch counters, gift shops, and gas stations were open to both races. Toilets were separate except at Lewis Mountain and Pinnacles. The Lewis Mountain camping area was mostly unused; the lodge had an occupancy rate of only about 5 percent, and the picnic ground about double that.

The Lewis Mountain area was completed just as Newton Drury— more inclined to end segregation than Cammerer—became director of the Park Service in August 1940. He immediately declared all picnic grounds open to both races. Equally decisively, he demoted Superintendent Lassiter to regional engineer and transferred him (over Senator Byrd's protest) to New Mexico. Nevertheless, the "For Negroes" sign remained at Lewis Mountain, as did the "White Only" sign at Big Meadows. Five years after the park's opening, the issue of racial segregation was far from resolved.

Wrangling over segregation came to a temporary halt during the early days of World War II, as overall park visitation declined dramatically. Lewis Mountain and Big Meadows opened for the 1942 season, but closed only two weeks later. The National Park Service itself was virtually shut down during the war, but still the debate over segregation in the parks continued.

Taking advantage of the lull, the Interior Department's adviser on Negro affairs urged that segregation be ended throughout the system, but the Southeast Regional Office queried a few parks and then discouraged any such move. Shenandoah's new superintendent Edward Freeland's views did not differ much from Lassiter's.

It appeared that the issue would have to be resolved at an even higher level, but President Roosevelt died in April 1945, and his New Deal administrators began to drift away. Needing conservative southern votes in Congress as Roosevelt had, President Truman was not eager to push civil rights. Interior Secretary Ickes, one of Roosevelt's stronger advocates for expanding civil rights, stayed in office until February 1946. His final official act was to abolish segregation throughout the Park Service.

But even Ickes's decisiveness did not fully resolve the problem at Shenandoah. Concessionaire Virginia Sky-Line balked at the order. Ickes was adamant, but his successor Julius Krug was willing to compromise. Through Senator Byrd, he worked out a plan for gradual change, and park facilities stayed segregated through the 1946 season.

As both domestic racial violence and international pressures grew after the war, President Truman began more aggressively to promote progress on civil rights. In June 1947, he proclaimed that the federal government must become "a friendly, vigilant defender of the rights and equalities of all Americans." He reasserted the principle in his 1948 State of the Union address.

Thereafter, no legal or policy grounds remained for continuing segregation in any form at Shenandoah National Park. The Lewis Mountain area and the dining room at Panorama opened for joint use during the summer of 1947, and following Truman's appointment of Oscar Chapman (a strong advocate of racial equality) as interior secretary in 1949, all remaining facilities became integrated. The 1950 season was the first completely integrated one in the park's history.

LEWIS MOUNTAIN AND THE PARK: WHAT TO SAY ABOUT IT NOW?

Staff changes in the 1950s robbed Lewis Mountain of some of its old magic and continuity, and new civil rights laws in the 1960s made other facilities available to African Americans. Use of Lewis Mountain—especially by local people—declined. Homecomings and Sunday School picnics moved elsewhere, drawn partly by the novel availability of swimming pools. At last, the "Negroes Only" and "Whites Only" signs disappeared.

The camp store holds many fond memories for visitors and employees alike who worked, socialized, played ping pong on the porch, and danced there in the years that Lewis Mountain was a "jumpin' joint!" *Library of Congress*

Still, the question remains how best to interpret and inform the public about Lewis Mountain's role in the park's history. Some of the "heroic" sites of the civil rights struggle in the United States have been marked: the Woolworth lunch counter in Greensboro, Kelly Ingram Park in Birmingham, the Lorraine Motel in Memphis, and others. Twenty miles east of Skyline Drive, in Orange, Virginia, stands the railroad station on James Madison's Montpelier estate, restored meticulously to its Jim Crow-era condition as a permanent reminder.

If it is wise to preserve and interpret such sites of the old "local customs" so that we can remember what Jim Crow was really like, how could Shenandoah National Park best do that?

The exhibit at Byrd Visitor Center (opened in 2007) endeavors to preserve the memory of all aspects of the park's past, including Lewis Mountain.

Chapter VIII

SHENANDOAH AND THE NATIONAL PARK
SERVICE DURING AND AFTER WORLD WAR II

When the National Park Service was created in 1916, it managed only forty-one units; its budget was only $3 million (in 1990 dollars), and fewer than 400,000 people visited the parks during the first year. By 1940, appropriations reached nearly $200 million, and there were nearly seventeen million visitors. During the New Deal years, the number of park system units had risen from sixty-five to 214.

Then came the war, and by 1944, appropriations dropped to only $34 million. The Park Service was left with only a third of its prewar staff, and many parklands and facilities (including some at Shenandoah) were turned to military uses.

Shenandoah's second superintendent Edward D. Freeland, who arrived less than a month after Pearl Harbor, found both the Park Service and the CCC already "crippled," but he hoped that wartime stress might actually increase visitation. Gasoline and tire rationing took their toll, however, and by May of 1942, travel was down by 75 percent.

The CCC ceased to be funded in July 1942, depriving the park of a large and dedicated workforce it had had since it opened. A hundred or so conscientious objectors (some of them skilled Mennonite craftsmen) repopulated the Pinnacles CCC camp in August and provided some needed labor power, but the flush days of the 1930s were over. Both Big Meadows lodge and Lewis Mountain soon closed, although campgrounds, picnic grounds, and trails remained open. Seeing their October 1942 revenues fall nearly to zero, Virginia Sky-Line asked (and was allowed) to reduce services.

Visitation at Shenandoah, which had topped 900,000 every year since 1937, dropped below 42,000 in 1943. It was the most dramatic drop (95 percent) experienced by any park in the system—probably tied to the importance of Skyline Drive to most park visitors, and wartime strictures against pleasure driving.

RIDE TOGETHER

WORK TOGETHER

SAVE RUBBER

FOR VICTORY

BALLINGER

PHILADELPHIA METROPOLITAN WAR TRANSPORTATION COMMITTEE

MAYOR BERNARD SAMUEL · ROBERT A. MITCHELL, ADMINISTRATOR

WPA

Rubber and gas rationing for the war effort put a stop to weekend road trips to Skyline Drive.

For most parks, a postwar upturn was at least as dramatic as the down-turn had been. As gasoline, tires, and new automobiles became avail-able again, Shenandoah visitation climbed back above 850,000 in 1947. It did not total more than a million again until 1949, but by 1952, it reached 1.5 million—severely straining facilities, staff, and budget.

Shenandoah and Skyline Drive were by no means alone in this regard. If the National Park system was to tolerate and serve such vastly increased numbers, the staffs, budgets, and facilities had to be expanded and upgraded quickly. Unfortunately, the Park Service budget in 1955 was slightly below what it had been in 1940, while overall visitation had tripled.

RECOVERING FROM THE WAR: MISSION 66 AND POSTWAR CHALLENGES

Fortunately, 1956 witnessed the beginning of a ten-year program called Mission 66. This program marked the fiftieth anniversary of the birth of the National Park Service in 1916 and aimed to improve and dramatically expand the parks' badly overstressed and deteriorated infrastructure.

Dealing with these stresses on the system by limiting use was briefly considered but rejected. "The parks belong to the people,"

The Skyland dining room (insert), part of the Mission 66 initiative, replaced the earlier more traditional-style dining hall that burned in 1948 (background). The newer Mission 66 buildings were criticized for their modernistic architecture. *NPS Archives*

Mission 66 guidelines said, "and they have a right to use them." Rehabilitating existing facilities and building new ones was thus the chosen alternative.

New park master plans were developed to respond to postwar developments and trends, and before the program ended, a billion dollars had gone toward the effort. Its effects were evident throughout the system in new roads and bridges, trails, parking areas, campgrounds, utilities systems, and buildings (including one hundred visitor centers).

Two of the new buildings built were the flat-roofed, glass-walled dining hall at Skyland that replaced the picturesque old one, destroyed by fire in 1948, and the Harry F. Byrd Sr. Visitor Center at Big Meadows (1963–1967). These two buildings (especially the Skyland dining hall) did not escape criticism leveled at Mission 66's modernist architecture from some quarters, especially from those who preferred the "park rustic" or "parkitecture" style long familiar throughout the system.

The grand opening (background) of Skyland was attended by numerous dignitaries including NPS Director Conrad Wirth (insert). *NPS Archives*

Superintendent Guy D. Edwards's objections to some aspects of the dramatic Mission 66 expansion were overruled, but time proved them to have merit. Visitation was rising rapidly, to be sure—from a wartime low of about 42,000 to 1.6 million at the beginning of Mission 66, but sustained increases as large as those predicted by Mission 66 planners did not materialize. Visitation rose to nearly three million in the post-bicentennial year of 1977, but fell to around two-thirds of that by the mid-1990s and continued to drop before leveling off at just over one million in 2005.

By many measures, however, the park thrived during (and beyond) the postwar years. When former chief ranger R. Taylor Hoskins, not having seen Shenandoah in twenty years, replaced Edwards as superintendent in late 1958, he was astonished by the densely re-grown forests and the proliferation of wildlife. Hoskins wanted to commission a geographical history of the park, to save buildings important to its human past, and to smooth out its jagged boundary by buying some additional lands, but no funds were available.

Succeeding Hoskins in 1972, Robert R. Jacobsen moved successfully to make the park much more appealing and accessible to backpackers, and to add about 40 percent of its acreage to the National Wilderness Preservation System.

Before retiring in 1986, Jacobsen engaged in a far-sighted attempt to address the newly emerging threats of air pollution and acid rain. Like other units in the system, Shenandoah continues to be threatened by invasive insects, plants, and animals. And during some recent years, smog and haze have been worse than at any other national park in the country—drastically reducing visibility, poisoning trout streams, and damaging plants and forests.

Pollution continued to rise through the early 1990s, as in fact it had for decades. Calling urgently in 2004 for regulatory attention to the problem, the *New York Times* hearkened back to the one-hundred-mile vistas George Freeman Pollock "raved and shouted" about from Stony Man in 1886—vistas now "lost in the haze," reduced to no more than twenty miles on an average summer day.

Like other national parks, Shenandoah has in recent years had to take a fresh look at its lands, facilities, and programs in order to conserve its natural and cultural resources, respond to a changing population of visitors, cope with fluctuating levels of funding, explore new technologies for information and interpretation, and meet rising needs for security.

During this period, news about the national parks has been characterized—as it has from even before there was a National Park Service—by passionate policy differences. When a high-level Interior Department official suggested in 2005 that protections against overuse and damage to the parks should be loosened, former Shenandoah superintendent Bill Wade disagreed sharply.

Such policy differences will continue as a part of the always complicated public discussion about our national parks. The challenge the park faces, as all national parks have since the beginning, is the original "dual mandate" of the 1916 legislation that created the National Park Service: to "conserve unimpaired" the legacy of land and resources, while at the same time providing for their enjoyment by as many visitors as choose to come.

SELECTED SOURCES

Books and Articles

Carr, Ethan. *Mission 66: Modernism and the National Park Dilemma*. Amherst, MA: Library of American Landscape History, 2007.

Davis, Timothy, Todd A. Croteau, and Christopher Marston, eds. *America's National Park Roads*. Baltimore: Johns Hopkins University Press, 2004.

Engle, Reed. *Everything Was Wonderful: A Pictorial History of the Civilian Conservation Corps in Shenandoah National Park*. Luray, VA: Shenandoah National Park Association, 1999.

———. *In the Light of the Mountain Moon: An Illustrated History of Skyland*. Luray, VA: Shenandoah National Park Association, 2003.

———. "Laboratory for Change." *Resource Management Newsletter* (January 1996), http://www.nps.gov/shen/historyculture/segregation.htm.

———. *The Greatest Single Feature: A Skyline Drive*. Luray, VA: Shenandoah National Park Association, 2006.

Horning, Audrey J. *In the Shadow of Ragged Mountain: Historical Archaeology of Nicholson, Corbin, & Weakley Hollows*. Luray, VA: Shenandoah National Park Association, 2004.

Krutko, Erin. *"Under the Sky All of Us Are Free": A Cultural History of Lewis Mountain, Racial Segregation, and African American Visitation in Shenandoah National Park*. Williamsburg, VA: American Studies Program, College of William and Mary, 2009.

Lambert, Darwin. "Administrative History of Shenandoah National Park," 1924–1976. Luray, VA: n.p., 1979.

———. *The Undying Past of Shenandoah National Park*. Boulder, CO: Roberts Rinehart/Shenandoah Natural History Association, 1989.

Lambert, Darwin and Reed Engle. *Herbert Hoover's Hideaway*. Luray, VA: Shenandoah National Park Association, 2011.

Paige, John C. *The Civilian Conservation Corps and the National Park Service, 1933–1942*. Washington: National Park Service, 1985.

Perdue, Charles, Jr. and Nancy Martin-Perdue. "Appalachian Fables and Facts: A Case Study of Shenandoah National Park Removals." *Appalachian Journal*, 7 (Autumn/Winter 1979), 84–104.

Powell, Katrina. *The Anguish of Displacement: The Politics of Literacy in the Letters of Mountain Families in Shenandoah National Park*. Charlottesville: University of Virginia Press, 2007.

———. *"Answer at Once": Letters of Mountain Families in Shenandoah National Park, 1934–1938*. Charlottesville: University of Virginia Press, 2009.

Salmon, John A. *The Civilian Conservation Corps, 1933–1942: A New Deal Case Study.* Durham, NC: Duke University Press, 1967.

Simmons, Dennis E. "Conservation, Cooperation and Controversy: The Creation of Shenandoah National Park and the Skyline Drive, 1924–1936," Ph.D. dissertation, University of Virginia, 1978.

The Negro Motorist Green Book. Published 1936–, under slightly varying titles.

Whisnant, Anne M. *Super-Scenic Motorway: A Blue Ridge Parkway History.* Chapel Hill: University of North Carolina Press, 2006.

Whisnant, David E. *All That Is Native and Fine: The Politics of Culture in an American Region.* Chapel Hill: University of North Carolina Press, 1983.

Online Sources

Ayers, Edward L. *The Valley of the Shadow: Two Communities in the American Civil War*, http://valley.lib.virginia.edu/.

Gilliam, George H. and William G. Thomas. *The Ground Beneath Our Feet: Shenandoah National Park*, http://www.vahistory/org/shenandoah.html.

New York Times historical newspaper archive.

Virginia Foundation for the Humanities. *Encyclopedia of Virginia*, http://www.encyclopediavirginia.org/.

Virginia Historical Society. *The Civil Rights Movement in Virginia*, http://www.vahistorical.org/civilrights/pec.htm.

Part III
EXPERIENCE SHENANDOAH TODAY

Shenandoah Today

In the years since Shenandoah National Park was established, millions of people have passed through its gates seeking respite, rejuvenation, and recreation. Some have driven only a portion of Skyline Drive, marveling at the views of the Piedmont and Valley. And some have backpacked deep into its wilderness to find solitude and to commune, uninterrupted, with the natural world.

The visitor experience at Shenandoah is as varied as the visitors themselves. Providing and protecting the unique Shenandoah experience for this and future generations has been the mantle passed from park manager to park manager through the decades. Since the park's establishment in 1935, additional protections have been sought and obtained. In 1976, 40 percent of the park's acreage became federally designated wilderness. In 1988, Rapidan Camp was declared a National Historic Landmark. And in 2008, the Skyline Drive Historic District including Big Meadows, Skyland Resort, and Lewis Mountain was established. Both flora and fauna have grown in diversity, making Shenandoah a haven for rare and endangered species as well as an environmental indicator for the East Coast.

The vast vistas from Old Rag Mountain reward hikers. *NPS/Robert Kuhns*

A white-tailed deer invites visitors into her home. *NPS/John F. Mitchell*

Whether the casual park visitor is aware of these protections and preservation efforts or not, the results are in the Shenandoah you visit today. The 105-mile Skyline Drive is the portal to your Shenandoah experience. Hidden in its curves and landscape, visitors will discover subtle markers indicating the locations of over 500 miles of beautifully wooded trails that lead to stunning waterfalls, fantastic vistas, or simply to serenity. Along the way, drivers, passengers, and hikers alike can see abundant wildlife in their natural habitat including white-tailed deer, black bear, and over 300 other species of mammals, fish, birds, amphibians, and reptiles. An overstory of predominately oak-hickory forest creates comforting shade and sustains life in the never-ending web of the Central Appalachian ecosystem.

Over 1,300 species of plants provide homes and food for both year-round and migratory residents. The sparkling night sky over Shenandoah is a magical treat, especially for urban dwellers.

Four campgrounds and three lodging facilities provide places to rest and regroup for the overnight visitor.

Don't miss the small things. *NPS/Ed Knepley*

Ranger activities bring kids (and adults) closer to Shenandoah. *NPS/John F. Mitchell*

Throughout the park there are havens for solitude. *NPS/ John F. Mitchell*

Opportunities to get to know your national park are everywhere in the exhibits, films, signage, and publications available throughout the park. Ranger programs in many of the developed areas of the park provide an added layer of opportunity to make special connections with the resources of Shenandoah. Join a ranger to discover the mysteries of Big Meadows or to meet live raptors and understand their place in Shenandoah.

To plan the perfect getaway to Shenandoah, visit the official park website: www.nps.gov/shen. Here you will find directions, downloadable hiking maps, information, links to campground reservations, and other important information. The Shenandoah National Park Association offers guidebooks, maps, and other publications at www.snpbooks.org. The park's concessionaire, ARAMARK (www.visitshenandoah.com), manages the lodges, restaurants, gift shops, and other visitor amenities. ARAMARK also presents a variety of entertainments throughout the season.

What will you discover in Shenandoah National Park? The unending horizon across the Valley and Piedmont? Or something much closer—a spider web made magical by a foggy morning or a tumbling waterfall rewarding a long summer hike? The hideaway of a president or the remnants of a Civilian Conservation Corps camp? Each visit reveals a new Shenandoah. Discover the past, explore the present, and be a part of the future of Shenandoah National Park.